5 Ways
to
Save the Planet

Key changes in beliefs and actions that will
solve our biggest problems

by

Gregory J. Schwartz, Ph.D.

This book is dedicated:

To the great geographers who served as my mentors and advisors:
Greg Knapp, Karl Butzer, and Yi-fu Tuan

To my wonderful parents, Jim and Faye Schwartz,
my genius sister, Stephanie,
and especially to my loving and amazing wife, Chanel

Taro Patch Small Press
San Clemente, CA 92672

Cover Image by Vicky Lee

BISAC Subject Headings:

SOC015000 SOCIAL SCIENCE / Human Geography
NAT011000 NATURE / Environmental Conservation & Protection
EDU015000 EDUCATION / Higher

Author's website: www.gregoryjschwartz.com

Table of Contents

Introduction

On a hot fifteen-hour bus ride through Malaysia in the late 1990s, my tee shirt stuck to my back, soaked with sweat. The inescapable tropical humidity and ubiquitous mosquitos made laundered clothes and a good night of sleep seem like distant memories. When the bus finally pulled into a rest stop at the crest of a small hill, I stepped outside and gasped. Miles of pristine rainforest stretched out in front of me as far as the eye could see. I took a deep breath and exhaled slowly, motionless.

The forest buzzed with the sounds of Mother Nature's life force. If you've never heard it before, the harmonized din of a rainforest's insects and birds is surprisingly loud – something akin to being at the starting line of a motocross dirt bike race. It felt like I was standing in the thriving, pulsing center of the entire natural world. In that moment, something ancient and familiar came alive in me and I realized that I was a living part of this magnificent natural scene, not apart from it. And it was deeply fulfilling.

This experience came in stark contrast to the preceding few days of the journey where I had seen large sections of deforested and scorched land being readied for cash-crop plantations and development. Within the previous month, I had passed through giant shanty towns that surrounded the region's biggest cities where millions of people lived in squalor.

It was then that it hit me: no matter who we are or where we live, we are a part of the cause of the world's problems and we also feel the effects. Cattle ranches and soy cultivation in Brazil are created in order to supply global demand for meat, while the related deforestation is generating worldwide climate change. The suppression of developing world economies by first-world lending institutions and transnational corporations is pushing these poor, skyrocketing populations to unsavory sources of income such as logging of primary forests, poaching of endangered animals, and the sex trade, which exacerbates deforestation, species extinction, and disease vectors. Resource over-consumption and a fostered dependence on fossil fuels leads to costly wars over resources. This drains national coffers and leaves less to spend on education, health, and the conversion to the next-generation renewable energy infrastructure.

Blissful ignorance of other nations and of our environment is no longer an option. Yet at some point in our routine of morning lattes and nightly internet streaming, many of us have somehow been lulled to sleep; meanwhile our beautiful planet is slipping away. We have allowed ourselves to be distanced from nature, believing that we are apart *from* the natural world rather than a living part *of* it. And all of us at times acquiesce to the illusion that society is a competition between "us" and "them," which allows us to support policies that dehumanize and mistreat our neighbors. Standing in the Malaysian rainforest, in that moment of clarity, I wanted to yell so loud that the entire world would wake up ... and change.

For two decades I journeyed through Africa, Central America, Europe, South America, the Middle East, and Southeast Asia, and I witnessed much of the world's beauty and dynamism: an expanding environmental and human rights consciousness, the globalization of culture and communication, a growing tide of international philanthropy, and a move toward sustainable energy and agriculture. Yet at the same time I gradually grew overwhelmed at the scale of human suffering and environmental harm that is going on right now on our planet: deforestation and wars over resources, rapid climate change, an international sex and drug trade, rampant starvation, an exploding global population, and entrenched corporate control over flows of food, energy, capital, and political power.

Understanding the causes of this degradation and suffering quickly became the focus of my academic research, my travel, and my writing and teaching. After several years, I came to comprehend something amazing about the world's plight: the solutions to our biggest problems already exist, and they have for quite some time. For instance, we have enough food for everyone on the planet, but one-third of all food produced spoils or is thrown away and over half of all corn grown on the planet is fed to livestock rather than starving humans. We eat so much in the wealthy nations that it is killing us, while 15,000 people starve to death every day elsewhere.

Likewise, fossil fuels dominate, but huge solar power plants were already fully operational 100 years ago, and more electric cars were on American roads in 1900 than gas-powered ones. The harmful climate change, pollution, loss of life, and skyrocketing financial cost of excessive dependence on fossil fuels was never necessary, and even less so now. So why do so many people continue to starve, and why do we insist on our unnecessary addiction to fossil fuels?

If we just passed out mosquito nets, as UNICEF and others now do, one million African children would not die from malaria each year. The same is true of inexpensive AIDS drugs. To that point, the yellow fever and cholera that has been eradicated from the industrialized world still unnecessarily plagues many poor countries. Moreover, some of us in the West choose to demonize groups in the Middle East and cultivate the omnipresent fear of terrorism, never considering that by invading the Middle East and killing hundreds of thousands of people in our quest for resources, we (Western nations) are stoking the very fire that burns us.

The majority of the solutions to our most critical problems are reasonable, simple, and they are already here. They have been within our grasp for many decades. We have the people power, the technology, and the logical solutions to solve our problems. All that we lack is the *decision* to implement change. Therefore, our main limitations are not tangible. What hinders us is not what we have or don't have, but what we think and believe.

The most common beliefs that hold society back are discussed in the next chapter. One powerful limiting belief, perhaps the most simple yet powerful of all, is that the world's problems seem too big to solve, and that if someone wants to help solve them, they don't even know where to start. To move past this first psychological hurdle, simply **do one small thing** and see what happens. For instance,

1) **Eating one organic carrot** per day for a year decreases your chances of getting several kinds of cancer by 5-10%, keeps two to three pounds of pesticides and twenty pounds of CO_2 from being sprayed into your local air and water, saves U.S. taxpayers about $100, and saves at least one person from developing asthma (1).

2) **Shortening your showers by only one minute** saves 1,000 gallons of water annually and keeps 240 pounds of carbon dioxide from being spewed into your local skies (2).

3) **Giving $1 a day to an organization that helps children,** you will feed and clothe a child in South Asia for his or her entire life, or you will pay the annual school fees of seven African girls for the duration of their entire education (3).

4) A family **NOT eating beef at just one meal** saves a tree from being cut down in the rainforest and frees up enough grain to feed over forty hungry people a meal. If you abstain from meat once a week, you lower your chances of acquiring colon cancer, lung cancer, breast cancer, and decrease your chances of developing heart disease, usually by five to ten percent (4).

5) **Carpooling or taking public transit just once a week** keeps 28,000 pounds of carbon dioxide out of the air and saves, on average, $288 annually (5).

6) **Installing solar panels on your roof** is now, in most cases, completely FREE, your electric bill decreases, you increase the value of your home, and you keep 20,000 pounds of CO_2 from being emitted every year (6).

7) Educating one girl in the developing world costs about $75 per year. In turn, that girl will usually educate her entire family; she will also have fewer children, and she will be less likely to be abused by a man (7). Moreover, as women's rights to education, voting, and property increase in a given society, many social indicators improve, such as a decrease in crime and infant mortality rates.

Doing one small positive thing breaks inertia and can have dramatic repercussions. In order to save the planet we don't need a superhero, a revolutionary leader, or even a miracle from above, though all three of those would help! Solving the world's biggest problems is actually well within our power as everyday citizens of the globe – all that's needed is that most of us take notice and take action.

In the process, it's essential that we address both the tangibles and the intangibles that are involved: both the way that we live each day and the beliefs that we hold. If we could summon that revolutionary leader to guide us, his or her real power would simply lie in the ability to inspire each one of us to care about the suffering that we know exists, and to do something about it. This shift is up to those who are aware and those who have the power to help. And by that definition, it is up to you.

Our Beliefs Are Our Only Limitation

"We cannot solve problems with the same thinking we used when we created them"

- Albert Einstein

Does recycling and driving fuel-efficient cars actually help the environment or are we grandiose to think that our lifestyle habits can actually affect this huge planet? If your neighbors, or a neighboring country, are rising up economically does that help you or hurt you? Do strict gun control laws make us safer or less safe? Is it right to feed and shelter the homeless? Well, in each case it depends on what we, as individuals, *believe*. What we believe about society at large determines our answers to these questions. The same is true in our personal lives. What salary truly reflects my worth as an employee? Is there love out there for me or will I remain alone? Again, this is based more on what we believe about ourselves than on some measurable approximation of reality. And normally our beliefs are based on very specific, poignant experiences and observations in our past. Once our beliefs are formed, we tend to focus on outward events that match with and reinforce those beliefs. This is called confirmation bias.

Why do I bring up the topic of beliefs in a book about saving the planet? Because our beliefs are the foundation for the actions that we take and the policies that we support. Beliefs are especially powerful when they go unacknowledged and reside in our subconscious. This is why great psychiatric researchers of the 20th century –

such as Freud, Pavlov, and Jung – focused on the subconscious as the quickest way to determine, and change, behavior.

As I wrote in the introduction, our main restriction as a planet is not that we lack something technologically or materially. What limits us is what we *believe* about the world, which keeps us from enacting the solutions that are already here. We have enough food, energy, and technological acumen, for instance, for all of us to live fruitfully, but we as a planet are mismanaging these resources based on several of our archaic beliefs. The world is constantly moving forward, but often our mindsets are not. Eminent scientist Thomas Kuhn was one of the first to introduce this idea of a "paradigm shift." He explains that essentially every major scientific breakthrough is preceded by a release of old thought patterns, former paradigms, and outdated traditions. So, in the quest to save the planet, changing our beliefs is just as important as changing our actions.

At countless times in history, outdated beliefs needed to be replaced by progressive, new ideas in order for the world to move forward. What shape would the Western world be in if the Greeks had not stepped past dictatorship and developed democracy? Who can imagine that only fifty years ago the United States passed the Civil Rights Act? And how did countless countries operate before women could legally vote? These shifts in beliefs were necessary and sweeping and they brought about changes, without which, our world is difficult to imagine.

There are a few broadly held beliefs – by billions of people – that are so limiting that they have held back society's evolution for centuries, or even millennia. One such belief is the idea that advancement is achieved through competition and conquest. Throughout history, civilizations have expanded and "progressed" by conquering others militarily and economically. This has been true from the Egyptians, Aztecs, and Romans to the Mongols, Turks, European colonizers, and modern day super-powers. While this belief has allowed some societies to grow and acquire wealth and resources, it has left, in its wake, destruction that has eradicated cultures, histories, and countless human lives.

What if we shifted to a different assumption – that advancement is achieved through collaboration and *interdependence*? Many mainstream authors and academic studies across the social sciences espouse this approach. This spurs us to strive for the best in all aspects of society, yet it lets us see that when we attack and harm our neighbors, we only harm ourselves. There is copious evidence of this reality, if we just look around. Helping our neighbors economically inspires innovations that move our businesses forward, and their citizens' expanded buying power creates new markets for our products. If we protect the environment in adjacent nations, their clean air and water eventually cycles its way into our water supply and the skies that we breathe. But when we abuse other nations and the environment, we enter a downward spiral where our suffering neighbors and depleted environment have less and less to share with us, and their problems erode the base of our future health and abundance.

The Secret, a landmark best-selling metaphysical book, is founded on this idea of initiating an upward spiral with positive thoughts or a downward spiral with negative thoughts. How does this particular act or thing affect your health, finances, spirituality, career, or the environment? Does it create an upward spiral or a downward spiral?

A second critical shift in mindset is the move beyond logic and reason and into compassion. It is often said that what separated modern man from the animal kingdom, and even from his prehistoric ancestors, was his ability to use logic and reason rather than just brute strength or animal instincts. In the 21st century, however, another leap in consciousness is now called for. What currently separates those who are healing the planet from those who continue to ignore and damage it is the ability to empathically *feel* the needs and struggles of others. This empathy is sourced in the heart and not in the mind. Ghandi, Martin Luther King, Jr., Mother Teresa, and John Muir embodied such empathy. Modern figures such as Pope Francis and even Senator Bernie Sanders do as well. Those who feel the pain of their neighbors and sense the needs of the planet display compassion, and are often moved to play a part in rectifying these ills.

Directly related to this is the third shift in thought in which a person transmutes from being self-focused to being globally minded. Self-centeredness precludes our ability to comprehend our individual impact on the world outside of us. The Western world was buoyed a few centuries ago by the European Enlightenment's ideas of individual rights and Adam Smith's notion that "selfish" economic actions will produce the most productivity and utilitarianism overall. These ideas did, arguably, move the world forward, yet the extreme income inequality and capitalistic degradation of nature in the 21st century signal us that a shift in our beliefs is definitely overdue. How does my lifestyle affect the air and the oceans and the forests? How do my choices affect people in other nations? How will my life affect the next generation, and the next, and the one after that? We must expand our world view spatially, to include other regions, as well as temporally, to consider future generations and learn from past ones.

This belief, then, is fundamentally based on the idea that everything is interconnected; our money, the environment, our physical health, and our spirituality are all parts of the same larger whole. A choice that helps in one aspect but hurts all others will not survive and flourish in our grander world future. For instance, environmentalists who don't include financial considerations in their proposals lack practicality. Those who follow strict religious doctrines yet do not care for God's green Earth nor their body temple would do well to examine the core foundation of their beliefs. And financial and industrial leaders who dismiss both the environment and the health of future generations in their decisions could find that their apparent short-term gains are sabotaging long-term prosperity.

This holistic perspective raises new questions. What is the economic value of *not* cutting down a grove of redwood trees? How much tourism money is made by *not* destroying a beautiful bay with the drilling of leaky oil wells? If we took the $2 billion *per day* that the U.S. spends militarily and used it to better educate our children, we would no doubt produce more scientists and diplomats who could better resolve our international conflicts rather than so often choosing the option of war. When we make holistic choices, we cultivate our true wealth and establish an upward spiral of abundance.

Fourth, it is critical to understand that beliefs and behaviors that are normal may not necessarily be beneficial. Said another way, just because something is familiar does not mean that it is natural or good (1). Some of the values that we have learned and adopted from our family, our culture, our religion, or perhaps our country may be outdated or harmful. For instance, the ideas and practices that we ingest through the mainstream news media, the mainstream food industry, and mainstream music and entertainment must regularly be questioned to assess if they match with values that we consciously subscribe to.

Fifth and finally, when encountering a new problem, from the personal scale to the global scale, we can often vacillate between worry and apathy without ever taking any action. Or as Al Gore suggests in "An Inconvenient Truth" – we jump from ignorance to despair without pausing in the middle to do something about it. Neither despair nor apathy produce good nor do they generate change. It is so very critical that we learn to inhabit that precious middle ground where we seek awareness of the world's problems, yet not become overwhelmed or just give up when we comprehend their extent. Ultimately it is very helpful when we accept our partial role in causing global-scale problems, then commit to taking even the tiniest steps toward solving them. This is conveyed by a popular Kenyan phrase "Kidogo Kidogo" (take it little by little). The power of doing one simple thing each day to help the planet was outlined in the previous chapter.

When these five limiting beliefs in global society are shifted and replaced with more empowering ones, the door will be opened for significant tangible changes in the real world. Our beliefs form the foundation of our actions and lifestyles, and they heavily shape our world view. On that topic, author James Arthur Ray presents a chart of the seven levels of personal identity that can help each of us see how we view ourselves in relation to others and the world around us. Every friend, student, and family member to whom I have shown Ray's hierarchy has found it eye-opening, so I hope you will agree. Below, I list a generalized summary of Ray's chart.

Level 1: INDIVIDUAL. The first level of awareness. Someone at this level is primarily concerned with their own well being, needs, and desires and has little care for other groups, other nations, the environment, animals, etc. The classic selfish, egocentric human being.

Level 2: GROUP. A person at this level is focused on a small group of people: a team, a gang, a clan, a neighborhood, or even a family. They display strong loyalty to this group and often defend it vociferously or even with physical violence. All others outside of this group are held in lesser regard. This level is characterized by a search for power through group identity and cohesion.

Level 3: GENDER. This level, slightly broader, is characterized by people who affiliate with one gender, to the exclusion of those of the other gender. This can entail praising and focusing on one gender socially and professionally, and/or the denouncing the other gender. This approach leads to strongly patriarchal or matriarchal societies.

Level 4: ETHNICITY OR RACE. Perhaps I'm Chinese and I see my culture and ethnicity as the most important part of who I am. I hold other Chinese people, male and female, in the same high regard, but I necessarily see White people, Latinos, Black people, and other Asian ethnicities as not on the same level as my group. My personal life, business life, and voting patterns revolve around promoting and protecting my group and their rights and advancement.

Level 5: NATION or CULTURE. This category of being is defined by membership in a broad group, for example "I am American," "I am Nigerian," "I am a Muslim," or "I am a Christian." At this level, one's connection to the world is beginning to broaden to include millions of others, yet still this usually entails holding those of other religions and nationalities in lesser regard.

Level 6: HUMAN BEING. Someone at this level holds in high and equal regard every single human being, regardless of race, religion, color, background, gender, sexuality, language, or other difference. They acknowledge the commonalities and kinship between all humans and no longer see the world as "us" versus "them" because everyone is now in the category of "us." They may, but do not necessarily, esteem animals or the environment.

Level 7: UNIVERSAL BEING. A person at this level sees that everything in the entire universe comes from the same abundant Source. This leads to the understanding that we are all one and that all people, animals, and things, both animate and inanimate deserve our respect and consideration. Realizing their connection to all, this person makes decisions with regard to all involved and all affected in any endeavor, law, business, or encounter (2).

Where do you reside on this hierarchy? It may have inspired and uplifted you, but also may have poked you on some uncomfortable discussion points. I find that most of us are a blend of a few levels on the chart, and that often we move to different levels when we are exposed to more life experiences. It can be an excellent tool to gauge our awareness and to remind us to keep our eyes open and continually broaden our horizons.

Damsel in Distress

Climate Change has our Mother Earth in Dire Straits

"I really feel that nature is trying so hard to compensate for man's mismanagement of the planet. The planet is sick – like a fever. If we don't fix it now, it's at the point of no return... The time has come. This is it. People are always saying 'Oh, they'll take care of it, the government will, they will,' .... They Who? It starts with us. It's us, or else it'll never be done."

- Michael Jackson, King of Pop, philanthropist, and environmentalist, in 2009 documentary "This is it."

Standing at around 8,000 feet in the Swiss Alps and gazing at the majestic peak of the Matterhorn, it didn't make sense to me that the massive glacier we were standing on hadn't melted more by late July. "It melts a lot in the summer but then expands in the winter," said our college-aged guide from the nearby town of Zermatt, "but it is smaller now than it was when I was a boy. It shrinks more every year." The year was 1990 and "global warming" wasn't a common term yet, but the experience caught my interest.

Six years later, I found myself in East Africa speaking to villagers and international aid workers from Arusha, Tanzania near the base of Mount Kilimanjaro. "The ice is disappearing," was the conclusion of one villager and itinerant climbing guide. He was correct, because today, sadly, Kilimanjaro's mighty glaciers are completely gone. The country of Colombia used to boast fifteen mountaintops covered by glaciers, while today only five remain (1). The story is the same around the world in that nearly all of the glaciers studied on earth have been shrinking for many decades (2).

Are global warming and climate change real? Yes, they are world-wide realities. I am an academic geographer, and among the scholars and scientists who study the Earth, there is an overwhelming consensus that climate change is real, pressing, and primarily caused by human activities. Only in the popular media has any uncertainty been cultivated. Melting polar ice and thermal ocean expansion is raising sea levels, animal species are going extinct at an alarming rate, warming seas are causing more severe storms, and precipitation is falling more sporadically, causing both floods and droughts.

What exactly is global warming? We are releasing carbon dioxide into the atmosphere in massive amounts by burning gasoline in our cars, burning coal for electricity, and burning rainforest. This carbon acts like a blanket within the atmosphere, which causes temperatures on Earth to rise. Making matters much worse is that, over the last few decades we are cutting down our forests at the rate of 35,000 acres per day (3), and since trees (and plants) are the only thing in existence which can clean the carbon out of our air, this is a recipe for massive environmental change.

The Intergovernmental Panel on Climate Change recently determined that earth's mean global temperature has risen by over 1.3 degrees Fahrenheit in the past century (4). This number may sound small, but if your freezer is set to 31 degrees Fahrenheit and everything is frozen solid, when the temperature is raised to just 32.3 degrees, suddenly everything melts into liquid. In many regions in the spring and fall, temperatures walk that fine line on the freeze/melt point and 1.3 degrees of difference stretched over months is making a world of difference.

Although cooling and warming cycles are normal for the Earth, a notable human-induced warming has never been witnessed before now, so its effects are quite unpredictable. It took millions of years to store excess carbon in the form of fossil fuels under the ground, yet we are burning and re-releasing them all within a few hundred years. This is causing the natural world to change very rapidly. For instance, global sea level rose six to eight inches in the 20th century (5), but most *conservative* gauges estimate that it will rise from two to four feet in the 21st century (6). Many well-established estimates are much higher.

This means that, in coming decades, hundreds of millions of coastal inhabitants will likely be forced to relocate, especially in low-lying heavily populated areas such as Shanghai, Bangladesh, the Netherlands, and the U.S. state of Florida. Also, warming is destroying countless plant and animal habitats, resulting in rampant species extinctions. The current rate of extinction of birds, mammals, reptiles, and frogs is occurring at 20 to 1000 times the normal "background" rate, depending on the region (7).

In my geography classes, I share with my students that animal migration patterns, food supplies, and feeding hierarchies (food webs) are being altered or eliminated, which, combined with pollution and deforestation, is tearing the fundamental fabric of nature. Because of these shifts, in only fifty years, we will be living on a different planet than we are today. In the words of authors William Antholis and Strobe Talbott, "If we do not start the process of mitigating climate change right now, our descendants, however skilled, will not be able to cope with the consequences" (8). In accord with their assessment, I do not jest when I suggest that you go see the rainforest and the planet's glaciers and endangered animals within the next decade or two – while they still exist.

Visiting forty countries over the past three decades of my life, I've been privileged to see some of nature's most dramatic and beautiful displays, which has fortified my love of this planet. In Costa Rica, I bathed in lava-heated hot springs with my family as Mount Arenal volcano erupted in full view only a few hundred yards away. In Kenya, I camped on the Serengeti Plain with Masai tribesmen, listening to lions and hyenas howling at night – then by day witnessing giant herds of grazing elephants and the necks of twenty-foot-tall giraffes reaching up to break the distant horizon. Free diving off of a fishing boat in the Pacific Ocean near the equator, I suddenly found myself surrounded by a menacing school of sharks, each eight to ten feet in length. They took turns swimming toward me, mocking an attack, and then darting away at the last moment. After getting over my initial reaction of acute primal fear, I realized that perhaps they just wanted a better look, or that they were just testing me and monitoring my responses. Either way, I suddenly felt relatively safe…. in the middle of a school of sharks!

Off the coast of Vietnam, I gazed down to the ocean floor through fifty feet of the clearest turquoise water I've ever seen, before or since. I've traversed the mountains of northern Thailand, navigated its rivers on a bamboo raft, and seen the nutrient-rich waters of the Mekong River fertilize its delta and grow enough rice to feed ten million people. I once ran for miles through thick Central American jungle like an animal, my eyes and ears trained on every incoming sight and sound, only to plunge, breathing heavily and profusely sweating, into the odd silence of an open, barren field which had been recently deforested.

I saw the pageantry and demonstrative transformation of the changing seasons in Madison, Wisconsin during my graduate school years – once swimming nearly two miles across Lake Mendota, and then walking over the same frozen lake in winter. Perhaps as preparation for this range of experience, I spent the first eighteen years of my life in the blissful perpetuity of southern California's unchanging climate: 72 degrees and sunny nearly all year round.

I am truly enchanted by this beautiful planet and all of its natural rhythms. I always felt a kinship with nature as a child, and traveling the world to see its diversity, beauty and dynamism has only enriched that love and appreciation. I have studied Geography for many years and now I teach this subject in college. Geography is the study of how the processes of the Earth affect human beings and also how human civilization affects the Earth. Having this background is, no doubt, why I feel so deeply affected by the way that nature is abused and disregarded around the globe out of ignorance and apathy, most often for simple monetary gain.

We have been so willing to bear the deeply negative social, environmental and economic ramifications of fossil fuel use, as if there is no alternative. Please take a moment to really absorb the gravity of the effects of using fossil fuels: climate change, acid rain, smog in every major global city, trillions in tax dollars spent on war, hundreds of thousands killed in wars, thousands killed mining coal each year (9), millions of gallons of oil spilled into the ocean every year, and terrorist retaliation for our oil-related military aggression. All of these negatives are not an intrinsic part of "normal" life; they are a result of using oil and coal. This is a fact that purveyors of these fuels have desperately tried, with great success, to hide from the world over the past century. Catastrophic spills of sunshine or military invasions in order to steal a nation's wind supplies, by contrast, are not common news headlines, nor will they ever be.

Renewable energies are the single most important tangible solution to the planet's problems. Once it truly soaks into our brains how remarkable and practical solar and wind power are, the transition will be very, very rapid. Most solar companies now install solar panels on your home absolutely free. Call one and see! Conscientiously voting on renewable energy initiatives can have a big impact as well. Local and national governments around the world will save trillions of dollars by receiving renewable energy at a fraction of the cost of traditional energy sources.

The U.S. alone spends about $300 billion to purchase electricity every year. Going solar would cut that to a fraction of the cost within ten years. Solving disease, starvation, racism, political corruption, and war may involve more complex processes and timelines – though they are certainly also ameliorable – yet global CO2 production can ostensibly be halved within a decade if we aggressively shift to renewables. And we must remember that the greatest impediment to this change is simply the well-funded resistance of oil, coal, and natural gas companies.

By some estimates, the primary cause of climate change is actually eating meat. Robert Goodland, former World Bank lead environmental advisor, found in his 2009 article with J. Anhang that the global livestock industry may contribute to as much as 51% to climate change worldwide (10). Cattle grazing and growing food to feed cattle are principal causes of deforestation, while less than ten percent of calories fed to a cow are eventually yielded as consumable meat, hence wasting massive amounts of resources and energy. Cow methane flatulence as well as the transportation of inputs and finished products in the livestock industry both also

22

play significant roles in greenhouse gas production. In short, changing how we eat and how we use energy are far and away the most effective ways to slow climate change.

Sometimes on a human timescale, these changes that are occurring in our environment are barely perceptible, but on Earth's timeline, they are happening incredibly rapidly. By way of our massive annual release of carbon into the air, we are recreating the conditions that existed 50 million years ago in the Eocene era. At that time, huge quantities of CO_2 filled our atmosphere, heating the entire planet, melting the poles, and causing radical climate change. Sea levels rose over 200 feet, floods and droughts ravaged the planet, and species extinctions were rampant. Fossil records show that it took about 150,000 years for the excessive carbon in the atmosphere to be reabsorbed (11).

But most who debate this issue have a more localized perspective, like John Hammil, who works in Wyoming's North Antelope Rochelle Coal mine – the largest in the U.S. – and an undisclosed industry executive who says that mining coal is so profitable that it is "like printing money." Unlike oil supplies, which are precipitously drying up, the U.S. has a 150 to 250-year supply of coal reserves at current usage rates (12). Burning coal releases proportionally more CO_2 than oil, along with toxins such as arsenic and mercury, so even as oil reserves slowly recede, long-term pollution from coal still looms large. In 2009, the entire world released about 59 trillion pounds of CO_2 into the Earth's atmosphere (13), the U.S. being responsible for over one-fifth of that total (14).

The reason that we are in such a fix, of course, is that half of the forests on the planet are already gone. Moreover, only about a fifth of original "old growth" forests remain, principally in Colombia, Venezuela, Suriname, Canada, Alaska, the Russian Taiga, and the Guyanas of South America. For instance, according to the National Park Service, a full 96% of the original old-growth redwood forests of the U.S. west coast have already been logged.

Pristine virgin forests have astonishing biodiversity and some of the highest levels of energy and energetic vibration found in the natural world. This elevated vibration could be described as nature's consciousness, the planet's intelligence, or the soul of Mother Nature. An excellent depiction of this beautiful essence is found in the motion picture, *Avatar*, now the best-selling movie of all time. The movie's "Navi" people are a part *of* nature, not apart *from* it, and their synergy with nature allows both their natural world as well as their culture to truly flourish. When we understand these precious ecosystems from this perspective, it is much more difficult to scoff at "tree-huggers" and hopefully more difficult to reduce our natural resources to pure economic commodities which are to be harvested, bought, and sold. In the words of Hilary Benn, U.K. Secretary of State for Environment, Food, and Rural Affairs, "The time has come for us to put sustainable development into action, for the good of our forests, the lives they sustain, the biodiversity they support, and the survival of our planet" (15).

Curtailing deforestation is absolutely paramount, and palm oil production has recently risen to become one of the leading causes of deforestation worldwide specifically in Indonesia and Malaysia where it is destroying orangutan and tiger habitats. Rainforest Action Network (RAN) has recently pressured companies such as Kellogg's, Mars, Hershey's, ConAgra, and Smucker's to adopt much more responsible palm oil production policies (16), while in 2010 Greenpeace was able to push Nestle to dramatically reduce its palm oil purchases from tropical plantations. Previously, a successful RAN boycott against Burger King convinced the company to cancel $35 million in beef contracts in Central America, which together with a boycott against Disney's tropically sourced paper products have slowed deforestation on multiple fronts (17).

Yet this problem isn't easily solved because there are many forces pushing for deforestation and only a few pushing for conservation. Poverty, population pressure, cattle grazing, cash crop plantations, oil prospecting, and selling timber are the principal causes of deforestation. One of the easiest ways for those living in wealthy countries to help stop deforestation is to eat less beef – especially from fast food restaurants. In other chapters I discuss how cattle grazing and growing crops to feed cattle are responsible for up to 40% of forest clearing in the Amazon.

Other immediate ways to help are to avoid buying products made with palm oil, and to cease buying tropical hardwoods (mahogany, teak and rosewood are no-nos, but bamboo is OK!) and to donate to an environmental NGO that specifically fights deforestation. Examples are the Rainforest Action Network, Rainforest Alliance, and Amazon Watch.

Legendary performer Michael Jackson's hit "Earth Song" was accompanied by a poignant music video, which manifested his open denouncement of global deforestation. In interviews as well, Michael was very vocal (pun *intended*) about his love of the natural world. As heard in his 2009 documentary "This is it," Michael stated:

"I respect the secrets and magic of nature. That's why it makes me so angry when I see that … every second I hear the size of a football field (of rainforest) is torn down in the Amazon. That kind of stuff really *bothers* me. That's why I write these kinds of songs… to give some sense of awareness and awakening and hope to people."

Thomas Jefferson once wrote that "the earth belongs in usufruct (trust) to the living… no generation can contract debts greater than may be paid during the course of its own existence" (18). The Earth provides for us without question or limit and now it needs our love and care in return. So whenever you can, take the steps that are manageable to you – conservation, voting, or donating – that can fight global warming and keep the planet healthy for the next generation.

The Source of Our Problems

How Attitudes of Myopia, Indulgence, and Desperation Are the Root of Our Conflict and Suffering

"Fear is the path to the Dark Side. Fear leads to anger, anger leads to hate, hate leads to suffering."

- Yoda, Star Wars Episode 1

One summer during the late 90s, I found myself traveling alone in East Africa. During a phone call home, I was urged by my mother to be careful because the U.S. State Department's website admonished of a war and political instability in the East African region. I instantly wondered where this war was going on, because there was no evidence of it in Kenya, where I was located at the time.

I had a suspicion that this talk of war was completely rumor. I quickly found out that the "war" was in Uganda, so I hopped on a bus and headed in that direction. Sure enough, just across the border in Uganda, a newspaper headline read "War Rages in Western Uganda." Curiosity surpassed reason and I boarded a bus to western Uganda. The farther west that I traveled, the more the rumors diminished. Finally arriving in Mbarara, the supposed center of the war, I found the town peaceful. One shop owner had heard of a small skirmish among "a few boys with guns" up in the mountains behind the village. I had already realized that there was, in fact, no war, but I had come this far and I wanted to complete this mission, so I headed up into the hills on foot.

Before long, I saw three men in military fatigues carrying M-16 rifles. I tried to obscure myself behind a tree, but it was too late. One of the men noticed me, alerted the others, and then walked directly toward me. Nowhere to run, I froze. The man stopped three feet from me and said "Go home," then turned and walked away. My desire to investigate this war quickly ended with that statement. I decided that that was a fitting end to my East Africa trip, so I took his advice, and a few days later I was home in L.A.

The point of the story is that we can't always trust what we hear or read in the media – even things that almost everyone agrees are true. Sometimes we need to search out alternative books, periodicals, voices, films, and even locations, in order to find the truth. Even though I found no war on that trip, it needs to be said that conflict to the degree of genocide is indeed occurring in Uganda. "Invisible Children" is an organization there that is pushing for change. Distortion or omission of information is one way that problems and their solutions are kept separate. John Mayer touches on this topic in his song *Waiting on the World to Change*: "And when you trust your television, what you get is what you got. Cause when they own the information, oh, they can bend it all they want."

Mindsets and beliefs have indeed proven to be more difficult to crash through than any physical barrier as the world has transitioned through racism, civil rights, sexism, and the yielding of dictatorship to democracy. In each case, fear had to be replaced with knowledge, exclusivity had to give way to understanding and inclusion, and those in power had to see that a more equitable system was better for all involved.

In this chapter we will examine how certain restrictive and widely held beliefs in the 1st world and the 3rd world are transmuted into very harmful actions which often result in conflict and suffering. In the developed, or wealthy, world, the seeds of our problems can be found in our attitudes of **indulgence, avarice, myopia,** and **apathy.** These are the source of countless activities that are harmful to the world. If you live in the West, be particularly observant of evidence of these attitudes and you may be surprised at how pervasive they truly are. Unnecessary fossil fuel burning and excessive trash production are causing global warming, while our often unbridled consumption drives the sex and drug trades, deforestation, continuous war, and horrific treatment of animals for food and fur. **Apathy** among citizens of the West helps to perpetuate starvation, disease and unnecessary suffering in poor countries. Relatively small lifestyle changes and a modest redirection of disposable income in the West could elevate the world's poorest to a respectable standard of living.

In developing, or poorer, nations the story is quite different. Harmful actions are engendered by unhealthy attitudes of **isolation, corruption, and desperation.** Mismanagement of international aid money by third-world dictators cripples relief efforts, while deliberate political and cultural isolation hampers long-term economic and overall development. Also, desperate measures to survive, such as voluntary and involuntary participation in the sex trade and rampant deforestation, are propagating the spread of HIV and destroying tropical forests. If you observe daily life in Indonesia, Uganda, or El Salvador, for instance, you will see and feel the palpable presence of these pernicious trends in attitude.

To be clear, the wealthy nations, also called the first world or the developed world, are comprised of the U.S., Canada, Japan, Australia, New Zealand, and most of the countries in Europe. China, Singapore, Taiwan, South Korea and a few oil economies of the Middle East are sometimes added to this group. In the U.S., specifically, a large proportion of politicians together with oil and coal company leaders (i.e. ExxonMobil and Duke Energy), food industry giants (i.e. Monsanto and ConAgra), financial institutions (i.e. Goldman Sachs and Lehman Brothers), pharmaceutical companies (i.e. Pfizer, Novartis, and Merck), and military contractors (i.e. Halliburton and Lockheed Martin) guide and control the vast majority of resources and money (1).

I single out these companies because they have extraordinary influence over our government and legislation. This is because so many of their employees formerly held powerful positions in the U.S. government, and so many powerful government officials used to work for these companies. Though this is open, public knowledge, it is rarely referenced. This revolving-door oligarchy employs much suppression of information, technology, and social awareness in order to maintain influence over tax revenues, money and food supplies, and the political process. Dislike of our growing "corporatocracy" is a sentiment that American Democrats and Republicans share. Even though the fight to save the planet is often perceived to be waged against these monolithic corporations, I don't believe that they are inherently bad or evil. I personally believe that they simply maintain a unilateral focus on profit, often allowing money and power to become ends within themselves, which skews their perspective. With small, critical adjustments in their goals, these companies could shift their considerable human capital and productivity toward much more benevolent trajectories, improving both their public image and, inevitably, profits.

On the topic of war, in a few Western societies and especially in the U.S., tax money is used for military invasions. This provides an avenue for government money to flow to private contractors. It also allows for occupation and domination of nations with desirable resources, such as oil, drugs, or minerals. The standard rebuttal to this notion is that a strong military helps protect the U.S. and the global order by suppressing "dangerous" leaders and nation-states. But if that were true, then our military would put troops in North Korea, Iran, or the genocides in Africa, instead of setting up shop for a decade in oil and mineral-rich – and comparatively non-threatening – Iraq and Afghanistan.

Tax money is also shifted from government to big business in the form of subsidies and tax breaks. The legalization of unlimited campaign donations from corporations, a 2010 Supreme Court decision commonly known as "Citizens United," only exacerbated this un-democratic practice. Before the 2010 ruling, conventional farmers and pesticide companies already received about $20 billion in subsidies per year, depending on market conditions, while the major petroleum companies receive around $4 billion every year, not to mention tens of billions in tax breaks (2).

Senators and congressional reps can now receive unlimited corporate donations in exchange for votes that support subsidies or lax environmental restrictions. This is simply the everyday reality of the political process in Washington – an everyday reality which Presidential candidate Bernie Sanders has brought to the public's attention perhaps better than any other individual. This small government/corporate oligarchy, not exclusive to one political party, is very powerful and has astonishing potential for good, but they are steeped in a fear-based mindset which makes them a malevolent force on the planet.

Many believe that well-chosen government subsidies are very important, in fact critical, to guiding society and the economy. This is the classic Keynesian economic view. Since the 1980s, the more common global economic strategy has been the neoliberal view, which favors very little government intervention in favor of free markets and unrestricted trade. Ironically, a large portion of government intervention into the U.S. economy in recent decades has been to subsidize industries that are ruining the environment, degrading our food supply, and destabilizing our financial markets. Using this method, we are funding our own demise, which is more folly and self-sabotage than either Keynesianism or neoliberalism.

The tangible solutions to the world's pressing problems are already here, and in some cases have been available for decades. But abundance for all means reduced profits and control for the few, so they will literally fight to the death to suppress solutions. Greed and myopia preclude the oligarchy's understanding of how their actions are damaging the environment and hurting the less fortunate. However, author Alison Symington, addresses the blatant oversight of the power elite when it comes to human rights in the following quote:

"Somehow, policy-makers and 'experts' have become adept at debating development as if it does not involve people, trade as if it is an end in itself, and international investment and production supply chains as if they are the only option. Most financial institutions and international economic actors talk of human rights as if they are unnecessary, purely political, confrontational, and really just a distraction from the important matters at hand. In fact, discussions often go on as if human rights do not exist, alternative models and values are absent and irrelevant, and by and large, humans and the environment are similarly irrelevant" (3).

Moreover, many doctors have come across natural, non-invasive and non-narcotic treatments for cancer, which have been wildly successful in curing several forms of the disease for decades. Haven't heard of these cures? That's because they threaten profits for the pharmaceutical industry as well as the allopathic (Western mainstream) medical establishment, so these doctors have been sued, maligned, attacked, threatened, and quite often put out of business. Are you skeptical, yet you know someone with cancer who could possibly benefit from one of these natural remedies with exceptionally high cure rates? Go to these websites: www.cancure.org/hoxsey_clinic.htm or http://gerson.org/gerpress/clinics/. Additionally, it may be eye-opening to watch the film "The Truth About Cancer."

Relatedly, most of us have heard of the International Monetary Fund (IMF) and the World Bank, but you may not know exactly what they do or how influential they are. Basically these are large banks, centered in Washington, D.C., that lend money to various countries in order to help them develop. The general stated goals of these institutions are to encourage development and reduce poverty, and they do often produce bursts of increased economic output, yet their methods for achieving this have been met with strong criticism.

When loans are given to poor nations, they are laden with heavy contingencies. These so-called "structural adjustments" mandate that receiving nations open up their markets to vastly cheaper products from Western corporations, and that they de-nationalize their businesses, making them available to foreign purchase. So, together with the World Trade Organization, the IMF, and to a lesser extent the

World Bank, present a unified commitment to the neoliberal economic model mentioned above. Neoliberal is a somewhat misleading name since it is based on "free" open markets, private ownership, export-focused development (reminiscent of colonialism), and huge reductions in a government's spending on social services for its own people. Many specific initiatives and individuals within these organizations have magnanimous intentions, which are in fact carried out, but the larger effect – when the environment, women, and the poorest of the poor are taken into account – is manifestly negative. To its credit, the World Bank has increasingly and explicitly shown sensitivity to these issues in the past two decades (4).

Under the thumb of these often oppressive organizations, these developing countries have skyrocketing populations coupled with beleaguered economies. This, not surprisingly, produces a palpable desperation, which is the dominant negative energy of the developing world. Academics call this "dependency theory" whereby wealthy countries survive and thrive by keeping poor countries poor. Adding to this, the startling escalation of the Earth's population is putting heavy pressure on resources such as food and clean water, and this is experienced most poignantly in the poorer countries.

Desperation amidst limited options for income in the developing world has led to literally hundreds of millions of people exercising one of the few options that they have left – to sell nature. Nature, in this case, takes many forms. As a part of the natural environment, people's bodies themselves are put up for sale in the international labor and sex trades. Logging and the sale of lumber, or deforestation, is another commodification of nature in the absence of other avenues for income, while animal poaching for valuable hides and horns also abounds. A rhino horn commonly sells for $10,000 or more in countries where the average annual income is one-tenth that amount. The natural fecundity of the land is also monetized through cash crop plantations, while even beautiful vistas, beachfronts and coastlines are for sale and often abused through the tourism industry.

Indonesia has opened its doors to Asia Pulp & Paper Company, which is cutting down its rainforest at some of the fastest rates on Earth just to produce toilet paper and disposable toy packaging. This is causing populations of Sumatran tigers to plummet, prompting Greenpeace's "Tigers or toilet paper?" campaign. Orangutans are also being decimated by Indonesian deforestation in order to set up palm oil plantations, which supply the food industry in the West. Encouragingly, many companies are doing the right thing, like Disney along with the top ten book publishers in the U.S., who signed a pact to stop using paper products sourced from deforestation.

During the 1990s, I personally witnessed deforestation in South America, Africa, and Southeast Asia. I had my first encounter with the sweet, putrid smell of smoke from burning tropical forest while traveling by bus through a section of southern Brazil. The smoke engulfed our bus for long stretches of the twenty-two hour drive from Iguacu falls to Sao Paolo. I didn't know at the time that I would be greeted by that same sickening smell of burning forest in countless other countries in the tropics.

This "nature for sale" does cause much harm to the natural environment, but it has great potential to protect and save natural areas. Conservation of wildlife and big game, as well as their natural habitats, increasingly translates into tourism income from safaris and funding support from environmental NGOs. Wildlife populations have rebounded in various protected areas in Africa and South Asia, while forest has recovered in small pockets of conservation in countless locations.

Two other prominent trends in the developing world are corruption and isolation. Zimbabwe, the Philippines, Myanmar, the Democratic Republic of Congo, and North Korea are examples of nations that have been profoundly stunted by power-hungry rulers who embezzle national funds and isolate their countries culturally and economically.

And this is where *we* come in – the general population in wealthy nations. Our awareness of global warming, government corruption, and the ills of the food industry is growing, which is encouraging. Activism toward "going green," calling for government transparency, and supporting sustainable farming, for instance, is expanding significantly. Yet most are distracted from cultivating a global awareness by over-stimulation and entertainment – from 400 cable channels and sensationalized "reality" TV shows to our daily coffee fix, info-tainment news, and the constant vague fear of a terrorist attack.

Over two decades ago, author Neil Postman wrote: "Our politics, religion, news, athletics, education and commerce have been transformed into congenial adjuncts of show business, largely without protest or even much popular notice. The result is that we are a people on the verge of amusing ourselves to death" (5).

Most of us in the West have a vague awareness of the suffering, starvation, environmental crises, and war that most of the world is experiencing, but **apathy** overpowers urgency and we implicitly hope that these problems will simply work themselves out. Apart from the growing faction of Western society that is aware and active, the status quo in the West is simply to do nothing about these problems. If you would like to join this status quo, it is very easy – simply rise and sleep each day and only concern yourself with your own existence. Albert Einstein said that "the world is a dangerous place, not because of those who do evil, but because of those who look on and do nothing."

Those in this portion of American society are in jeopardy of becoming the next idle American or, if you will, the next American Idle. Rather than being an American Idol singing star, they couple their sedentary lifestyle with their idle mindset and simply observe as their own health and the health of the planet deteriorates. It is my hope for those on the brink of becoming the next American Idle that they will become a true idol and leader by using the privilege of living in the world's most powerful country to take action – with their votes, their money, and their lifestyle choices – to change the world for the better on behalf of their fellow man.

The Source of Our Solutions

Compassion, Responsibility, and Interdependence

"[Disease], hunger and food insecurity are injustices, with national and international institutions and actors significantly responsible. In other words, they are largely preventable and solvable problems, if human will is there to resolve them."

- Alison Symington, *Defending our Dreams*, 2005

Many years ago in Southeast Asia, I became fast friends with two Brits named Roger and Nigel. They were easy-going, likable guys, so we spent a few weeks traveling through the region together. We soon found ourselves on Tioman Island, just northeast of Singapore in the South China Sea, and the experience that we had there changed the way that I look at the world forever.

Stepping off the ferry that brought us to the island, it was clear that it had been only minimally developed for residences or tourism in any way. The island was large, mountainous, and covered in thick jungle – truly a place that was away from it all. The owner of the small structure near the beach where we were staying mentioned that there was a hotel and a restaurant on the other side of the island. The only way to get there was to wait for the bi-weekly ferry boat or to hike over a jungle-covered ridge of hills and down to the other side of the island. Zealous and young, we opted to take the challenging hike, which the owner said would take "a few hours."

41

We set out the next morning without packs or supplies, thinking we would buy whatever we needed once we arrived at the hotel, likely by noon. Hiking uphill, through jungle, and in the tropical sun and humidity proved a bit more of a challenge than we had anticipated. Two hours into the hike, we still had not even reached the crest of the hills, which we would then need to descend on the other side. Our intermittent chatter gradually grew silent as we could sense the growing danger that we were lost, battling oppressive elements, and on an island that was essentially uninhabited. And being lost in the jungle is not like any other experience of being lost. You can walk literally thirty feet, then turn around and have no visual clues as to where you just came from. As time passed, I began to imagine what creatures would be roaming this jungle when night fell and how we would defend ourselves. Just as the sensation of fear had most certainly overtaken the feeling of adventure on this sojourn, we came into a small clearing and what we saw changed everything.

In front of us were a man, whom we later found out to be Dutch, and his son daintily pulling nets through the air in attempts to capture and photograph butterflies. Roger, Nigel, and I all stopped – profusely sweating and exhausted – and stared at the two naturalists incredulously. Even before any words were exchanged, I immediately felt the stress drain from my body, based simply on the fact that this father and son clearly perceived there to be no danger nor cause for worry due to our isolated location. I finally spoke and asked the man if he had any idea how to get back to civilization.

"I know exactly where we are," the man responded. "I know this island like my own backyard!" Gesturing, though keeping his eyes trained on a butterfly, he said

"Just keep going in that direction over the crest of the hill and you'll hit the beach in a few miles. Then follow the beach north until you see the hotel."

His superior awareness of the island and his calm *knowing* that everything was going to be all right made our worries vanish instantly. About an hour later, we arrived at the hotel, safe and sound. What stayed with me from that encounter was how profoundly one person's experience and peaceful attitude can transform all of the people around him. It showed me the power of knowledge and deep awareness in times of crisis or fear. And many places on the planet, each in different ways, are experiencing crises or chaos right now. Armed with some rudimentary wisdom of global issues, and how to begin to solve them, each one of us can become that knowledgeable, calming entity that conciliates and transforms those around us. We can each be a guide to others and a presence that lets those in need know that even in trying times, everything is going to be all right.

It is amazing how often we have the opportunity to be that assuaging, reassuring presence, especially if you live in a wealthy nation. In the developed world, compared to those in poor nations, each of us has enormous power, resources, food, technology, and money. Each day we can use that power and capital to indulge ourselves, or to help others. The crazy thing is that most of us do neither, because we don't realize how much power that we actually have.

Maybe you, holding this book right now, will be the answer to the next prayer that cries out to the world from a small village in El Salvador or Mali or Bangladesh. You could be that knowing, calming presence that lets them know that everything will be all right. Perhaps you will decide to donate just $25 or $50 to an organization that helps provide medical care and or food in a beleaguered region.

And maybe that gift will end up saving a life, or ten lives, or feeding an entire family for a month. The compassion that I trust you feel in your heart right now is the most important ingredient in our present and future success as a planet. Seeing another person or group in need and allowing the **compassion** in your heart to move you to action – this simple idea is at the core of solving the world's problems. The other attitude at the core of our solutions is **awareness,** because this experience is usually followed by **responsible** action.

Many of us still have not fully adjusted to the idea that by uplifting our neighbor, we also uplift ourselves. If a country is thriving economically, their citizens and institutions have money to buy our products and services, which in turn helps our economy. They also have less need to abuse the environment, because with money and technology, budding nations are free to pursue renewable energies as well as sustainable development and farming.

Think how many nations have already benefitted from American ingenuity and technology. Our advancements in transportation, communication, disease prevention, computer software, and entertainment have made the world a more efficient, more connected, healthier, and at times happier, place. And the youthful nation of the United States, of course, rests on the shoulders of countless other long-established cultures, which moved global society onward and upward in its march through the centuries. The Chinese invented gunpowder and the compass. Germans made the first cars, the printing press, and initiated the development of Aspirin. Where would the world be if these inventions were not shared? The English discovered penicillin and they were the first to understand the human circulatory system as well as the first to smelt steel. Reaching into antiquity, many critical steps in the initial development of mathematics, language, and astronomy came from the African and Arab worlds. Samba and the Tango began in Brazil and Argentina, respectively, while Austria gave us Mozart, Freud, and Arnold Schwarzenegger!. And is there any country on Earth that has not in some way been influenced by the sophistication of French food, art, and philosophy?

The case could certainly be made that the world has benefitted more from collaboration than from conquest. This sharing and mutual uplifting has always moved society forward. Now that the world is so interconnected, this uplifting comes increasingly in the form of individuals and organizations in developed-world nations that help the developing world and help to heal the environment. Yet before these problems could be fully addressed, an expansion of global awareness had to make the problems known. That is, the "haves" had to become aware of the "have nots." Advancements in communication and transportation, as well as the globalization of culture and business, helped to achieve this end.

This increased knowledge of the world spurred individuals, organizations, and governments to offer help to the newly identified regions of need. Wealthy philanthropists such as Ted Turner, Oprah Winfrey, Bono, Helen and Swanee Hunt, Richard Branson, and Bill Gates have set a precedent for private benevolence with altruistic agendas that go beyond traditional governmental aid. Non-governmental organizations such as Amnesty International, UNICEF, Habitat for Humanity, the Red Cross, World Vision, Greenpeace, OXFAM, Medecin Sans Frontieres (Doctors Without Borders), and literally thousands of others have taken it upon themselves to move the globe in a new direction and show compassion, sometimes even in the face of much resistance.

The United Nations is undeniably the most important benevolent organization on the planet whose effects of nuclear disarmament, peace-keeping, and human-rights assurance are changing the course of global societal evolution. Many nations in Europe offer support for the environment and are joined by the United States in their international protection of human rights.

There are many avenues for this philanthropy. Almost one billion undernourished people on Earth and the several hundred million without adequate shelter need short term aid in the form of food, housing, and medical care. Disaster relief, such as the deluge of assistance that poured into Haiti after the giant earthquake of 2010, is a good example. Long-term projects include digging wells for drinking water, building infrastructure such as schools and highways, and setting up human rights abuse-monitoring organizations.

Nature itself is the other main recipient of this love and aid. Organizations like the Sierra Club, Greenpeace, The Nature Conservancy, and the World Wildlife Fund have been protecting the environment and animals for several decades. Their influence ranges from protecting the Arctic National Wildlife Refuge from oil drilling to preserving the habitat of orangutans in Indonesia to lobbying governments about international pollution reduction agreements. Their modus operandi, equally broad, includes grassroots volunteerism, regional environmental education promotion, and international advertising campaigns. Individual philanthropists have also had an impact on the environment. Ted Turner is a true environmentalist, donating hundreds of millions to environmental efforts in his lifetime. Richard Branson, owner of Virgin Airways, has pledged three billion dollars of his company's profits to help fight global warming.

One inevitable shift in coming decades across the entire planet – in both rich and poor countries – is how we produce energy and food. Approximately three-fourths of the world's energy is generated from burning fossil fuels which pollutes our air and water and is causing significant climate change. Renewable energies such as solar, wind, and geothermal are clean and also vastly cheaper in the long-term than fossil fuels. In terms of how we grow food, the past 100 years has seen the widespread use of chemical pesticides, chemical fertilizers, and genetically modified seeds. This increases crop yields yet annually injects massive amounts of toxins into our soils, waterways, and food chains which is resulting in giant aquatic dead zones, elevated cancer rates in humans, and polluted, depleted soils on an epic scale. Returning to organic agriculture techniques – a trend that is sweeping the globe – eschews these negative side effects.

Uplifting women is a powerful solution to a wide range of social problems, and it must become a broad effort that knows no socioeconomic or national boundaries. To say that women are oppressed is a huge understatement. At least one out of every three women around the world has been beaten, coerced into sex, or otherwise abused in her lifetime (1). Moreover, domestic violence causes more death and disability worldwide amongst women aged 15-44 than war, cancer, malaria, and traffic accidents combined (2).

I am shocked each time I read these statistics, and so we must continually repeat, reinforce, and refresh our efforts to improve the lives of women everywhere. We can do this in our personal lives with small decisions every day, and also we can support organizations that fight for women legislatively, politically, and socially. Several of these organizations are listed in the introduction to this book. A few more are "Womankind Worldwide" and "Pro Mujer." Also, www.delicateforest.com is a website that sells products made by formerly trafficked and exploited women and children.

Aid to the developing world is allowing inhabitants and nations who are buffeted by hard times to get back on their feet. When these poorer nations become more self-sustaining, healthy, and productive societies, they can begin to give to the world their true gifts, their unique contribution to the global, cultural and economic potpourri. For instance, a focus on community-based identity and problem-solving and symbiosis with nature can be communicated from the developing world to the developed world where more of a return to this foundation is needed. In this way, less developed nations can serve as the "roots" of global society, while the technology, "open" societies, and cultural and religious tolerance of the first world can be the "wings."

Likewise, governments and corporations can continue to broaden their goals beyond pure financial indicators to care for our invaluable natural resources. From this new perspective comes the realization that we are all a part of the same larger whole. So what began with core attitudes of compassion and awareness evolves into feelings of love and acceptance *for* every human, *by* every human, and a conscious collective decision to remain in a state of appreciation and harmony with the Earth.

Why is the Planet's Population Exploding?

What's ONE thing that you can do?

The single best way to slow population growth is to educate and empower women in the developing world. Giving them more rights and knowledge, better health care, and the power to determine their own future tends to dramatically reduce birth rates. Donating to women's organizations is the best way to affect this change (see "Uplifting Women" chapter).

In 1930 the Earth's population had finally reached two billion people. By 1960 that number doubled, and by 1995 it doubled again. It had required the entirety of human history for the population to reach two billion people and then in approximately one human lifetime, it went from two billion to six billion people (1). Most mid-range estimates predict that our population will peak at anywhere from nine to eleven billion inhabitants within the next century.

So what is causing this astronomical rise? The short answer is that birthrates have been high for thousands of years, but advances in medicine and the food supply mean, simply, that fewer people are now dying. The real crux of the issue is this central question: Why have the inhabitants of some countries urbanized, dropping their birth rates, while most of the world's people still live on farms in rural areas which keeps birth rates very high?

Walking the streets of Los Angeles, Chicago, Paris, or Tokyo, it may be difficult to see or palpably feel this global population explosion on a daily basis, but set foot in Sub-Saharan Africa, Central America, or central and South Asia and I promise, you will have a different window unto the world's condition. For instance, at current growth rates, Niger, Ethiopia, and Guatemala double their national populations about every twenty-five to thirty years. Spending time in many such nations, little by little, I became overwhelmed at the immensity of this issue. Interestingly, my reaction was the same when I first taught in the inner-city public school system in California. In both situations I thought to myself, "there aren't nearly enough resources for this number of people." This prodigious growth is transforming the natural world, as well as the way that we will live our lives from now on. Life on spaceship Earth is changing fast, and many more of us need to get out of the passenger seat and into the driver's seat if we are to turn the ship around in time.

The main concern related to the rising number of human beings is that all of these new people require water, food, and energy, while many of these resources are finite. Accessible fresh water supplies are actually decreasing due to glacial melting and overdrawing of groundwater, fossil fuels are rapidly running out, and the amount of arable (farmable) land on the planet shrinks every year due to desertification, over-farming, and expansion of cattle grazing. Wars are being fought at this very moment over oil, but even more fervor will charge the conflicts of the future over water, with thirty-one countries already facing critical fresh water shortages.

For most of human history – some 200,000 years – the population of the planet hovered steadily below a half billion people. In the late 18th and 19th centuries improved medical knowledge and more reliable food supplies (due to availability of new crops via international trade) both helped death rates to plummet, initiating a sharp rise in global population. During the next century, several Western nations industrialized, their people moved from farms to cities, and the expenses and education of urbanism made birthrates fall. This dramatically slowed or halted population growth in these countries. Yet most of the world has not made this final transition to industrialized urban life, so populations continue to escalate rapidly since a rural, agricultural lifestyle carries huge incentives for having multiple children.

These inchoate nations see their populations continue to vault at upwards of 2% per year, meaning they double in size about every 35 years. This includes most of Latin America and Africa, much of the Middle East, and southern Asia. People in these countries are also moving from rural to urban areas in such large numbers that it constitutes the largest migration in human history. But these migrants are not being pulled to cities by industry and jobs; rather, they are being pushed from country-sides, which are no longer able to support such enormous and growing populations.

The result is the emerging presence of giant slums or squatter settlements outside of megacities throughout the developing world. Cities like Mumbai, Sao Paolo, and Mexico City hover near twenty million inhabitants. Delhi, Rio de Janeiro, Dhaka, Manila, Seoul, Karachi, Cairo, and Kolkata (Calcutta) are close behind and growing fast (2). These cities are little more capable of dealing with these destitute masses than are the rural areas. Rural emigrants simply cluster into makeshift settlements on the outskirts of urban areas with informal housing, no sewage or electricity, and normally without paved roads.

I came across these makeshift settlements, or "favelas," in Sao Paolo and Rio de Janeiro in 1996 as I was traveling from Iguacu Falls up the east coast of Brazil by bus. Approaching both of these Brazilian megalopolises from their hinterland, our bus first encountered mile after mile of shanty-towns with shelters made of cardboard, plastic sheeting, corrugated metal, and the occasional cinder-block structure. These vast agglomerations seemed to have no end, with the city proper only a distant sight. A visitor entering and exiting the city through the main airport doesn't ever have to pass through and experience these parts of megacities where the least fortunate on our planet reside.

As evinced in the films *Slumdog Millionaire* (set in Mumbai) and *City of God* (set in Rio de Janeiro), these slums are riddled with violence, drugs, and deplorable sanitation conditions. The favelas of Rio are said to have the highest murder rates on Earth. On the other hand, favelas are also the source of burgeoning new culture, mostly in the form of art and music.

Due in large part to their rapidly expanding slums, several cities in Africa are growing at close to 4% per year, meaning their populations will double in less than twenty years. Dar es Salaam, Tanzania; Nairobi, Kenya; Luanda, Angola; and Kinshasa of the Democratic Republic of Congo are examples. It is a relatively simple equation that more people living off of the same resource base equals fewer resources per person.

A friend of mine in Kenya named David, who considers himself to be middle class, once shared with me exactly how much money he spends in one month. After paying for rent, food, transportation, entertainment, and some miscellaneous expenditures, he told me that he usually spent about $50 U.S. (4,500 Kenyan Shillings) per month. That's about $1.60 a day. Meanwhile, in the West, we are literally choking on our over-abundance of resources. Many of our leading causes of death – heart disease, cancer, and diabetes – are caused in large part by our cultural habit of simply eating too much food. Meanwhile, Public Storage, a company created solely to store our voluminous unused *stuff*, profited close to $2 billion in 2010.

This disparity is not a surprise to some. In 1798, English Parson and economist Thomas Malthus made a famous proclamation that since people multiply geometrically (1,2,4,8,16, etc.) while agricultural production multiplies arithmetically, (1,2,3,4,5, etc.) the Earth would soon encounter an acute scarcity of food. As testament to this prediction, currently on the Earth, some 15,000 people die of starvation every day, while forty-eight countries comprising 2.8 billion people are expected to face fresh water shortages by 2025 (3). Moreover, 40% of the world lives on less than the equivalent of US $2 per day (4). So this prognosticated "Malthusian Crisis" over limited resources has certainly arrived. But, as counter-theorizer Ester Boserup predicted, this crisis has been mitigated and delayed by advancements in farm technology such as the green revolution of the 1980s, which employed genetically engineered seeds and heavy chemical inputs in order to increase yields – sometimes up to three-fold (5).

Bill Gates continues to fund such projects which have the mixed result of producing more life-saving food, yet indenturing farmers to pesticide and fertilizer-company loans. Food output has increased so significantly that throughout the past century, famine is more commonly a result of political power-plays and failed distribution than of insufficient production (6). In fact, about one-third of all the food produced worldwide spoils or is thrown away annually, according to UN food czar, Jose Graziano da Silva. This is all the more troubling when we consider how many people unnecessarily starve to death daily. Yet, the massive chemical inputs necessary to increase yields have unfortunately left millions of acres of soil heavily polluted or depleted from over-farming, which threatens future harvests. A harmony must be attained between the sustainability of organic farming techniques and the soil-polluting yet high output Gates-funded green-revolution technologies.

Though great strides in our husbandry of resources are necessary, even perfect husbandry of our soils and resources will not totally solve our food and resource supply problems. The heart of this issue lies in the regions of the world that are still under-developed, comprising two-thirds of the planet, where populations are soaring. It becomes clear that helping these nations to economically evolve will allow their populations to successfully urbanize and their growth rates to finally slow down.

Yet it is precisely the economic and industrial rise of the third world that first world capitalists and industrialists quite actively eschew, because simply, this invites competition (7). With its myopic and necessarily short-term goal of profit, it is antithetical to traditional capitalism to support the success of one's "competitors." Yet environmentally, socially, morally, and collectively, it makes perfect sense – urgent sense – to indeed aid these economies and nations to progress. Corporate leaders together with organizations like the IMF and World Trade Organization have the responsibility of taking *care*, rather than taking advantage, of the world's resources and people. These players have been ambivalent about this calling, at times proving to be wise and selfless yet more often myopic and self-serving.

The notion of progress must be expanded beyond economic indicators to take in the survival of species, natural environments, and human cultures. It is too easy to decide from a table at Starbucks or a corner office with a view to "prudently" advance American interests globally and allow the prosperity to "trickle down" to those in beleaguered developing-world regions. If corporate and industry leaders witnessed the human struggles on the streets of Mumbai, Jakarta, or Nairobi, I do believe that compassion would begin to infiltrate their decisions and policies. Thankfully, environmentalism and philanthropic collaboration are rapidly emerging as dependable avenues to larger corporate profits. That is, helping your competition helps your bottom line: profit.

The rising population of the globe is a critical and pressing problem. Hopefully, our increasing inter-connectedness will continue to manifest and we will individually, nationally, and collectively take action to slow population growth and claim our grander future.

The Other Side of America's Wars

"One does not establish a dictatorship in order to safe-guard a revolution; one makes a revolution in order to establish a dictatorship."

- George Orwell

What's ONE thing that you can do?
Look up your local congressional representative and send him or her an email politely and honestly letting them know how you would like your tax dollars spent. If you would rather have military money spent on schools, infrastructure, and social programs here at home, tell them that. That is the bedrock of democracy.

My father joined the Marines and rose to the rank of Sergeant within two years, which is practically unheard of. By the time I was five or six years old, after I took a bath and got dressed he would ask me "What are you?" and I was trained to exclaim, "I'm a clean Marine!" I can remember him teaching me hand-to-hand combat techniques in our hallway before I went to bed.

My dad is probably the toughest, hardest working man that I've ever met, part of which he owes to his time serving in the U.S. Marines. He grew up on a farm in western Nebraska with its fair share of back-breaking labor, and all of his brothers, my uncles, also served in the military. In WW II, my Uncle Kenny served in the Navy, and my Uncle Keith trained pilots in the Air Force. While storming the beach at Iwo Jima, my uncle Harold lived through being hit by a grenade and stabbed by an enemy's bayonet. Sadly, my uncle Donny, whom my dad says was a lot like me, was flying a fighter plane in the Korean War that went down over the Pacific Ocean and was never found.

I was raised in a strong family, with a solid respect for our military and what it represents. As I grew older, it seemed that our military became increasingly active abroad, always finding a reason to be in the Middle East. The military became our most common tool of diplomacy, and its honorable purpose and ethos had been diminished by rumors that they were just fighting for oil. I began to feel that the military that I had been raised to respect was being both overused and *mis*used by our leaders. Somehow over-militarization had become interwoven with our national identity.

Right now America is in a significant economic recession with massive funding cuts in education, health care, the environment, and programs for seniors and children. In this fiscal environment, only one federal budget item was increased for the coming year: the military. We already spend around $700 billion on the military each year, which is 20% of our entire national budget, yet our representatives decided on July 9, 2011 to devote an additional $17 billion to our armed forces the following year (1).

The United States generates a phenomenal amount of economic activity – about $18 trillion annually – which is almost double the world's second largest economy (China). Yet our government is deeply in debt, to the point of crisis. The numbers just don't add up, because, essentially we have a spending problem. We currently spend more on our military than the next twenty highest-spending military countries on earth combined. Largely due to our military spending spree, our national debt has gone from $1 trillion in 1980 to $19 trillion in 2016. Though he was a great leader, Ronald Reagan's nuclear warfare program tripled the national debt in eight years. We now have 12,000 nuclear warheads, which are as big as or bigger than the one that was dropped on Hiroshima. Wars in the Middle East were the principal cause of taking the debt from $5.7 trillion to $10.4 trillion beginning in the year 2000 (2).

And this script continues today. I read the other day that the U.S. government is considering buying another fully equipped aircraft carrier, even though it will cost $15 billion. That is enough money to erase the 2011 budget deficits of Texas and New York combined, and it's more than the entire federal allotment to repair New Orleans after hurricane Katrina. And here's the thing – according to *Time* Magazine writer Mark Thompson, the U.S. already has eleven aircraft carriers, and it's very rare that we actually use them in combat (3). What's more, no other nation on Earth has more than one aircraft carrier. Do we really need a twelfth?

Just to provide some scale, the $15 billion cost to build the new warship is equal to the total profit earned last year by Walmart, the world's largest corporation. If we saved $15 billion by not building this one new aircraft carrier, that money would create remarkable change in other parts of society. For instance, it would re-hire almost *half a million* police officers, fire fighters, and school teachers for the coming year who have been recently laid off. Imagine how much safer and more enriched our cities would be if that came to pass.

If we had not purchased just three of the costly war ships, according to rough World Health Organization estimates, we could have fed every hungry child on Earth for an entire year. With that same $45 billion, the entire state of Florida could have been converted to 100% solar-power, saving the state $1 billion in electricity costs every year *FOREVER* and drastically shrinking their carbon footprint. Just for argument's sake, if we hadn't built any of the twelve giant warships, the U.S. could have relieved the whole continent of Africa of half its total foreign debt.

And remember, the $15 billion for one aircraft carrier is only 2% of the annual U.S. military budget. Let us, together, just imagine right now how dramatically the world would be improved if we decided, voted, and even demanded that more of that money, from *our* taxes, be used to benefit society rather than to destroy it.

We currently have over 500 military bases worldwide and some 75,000 troops in Europe alone. That's about the same number of U.S. troops that attacked Hitler's forces in Europe on D-Day, the largest amphibious invasion in the history of the world. Did I miss the memo, or why do we still need so many troops there?

One reason that we spend so much on war is that the Pentagon is staffed with over 900 high-paid generals and admirals who are helping to call the shots (4). They are the leaders of the military, so naturally they will see fit to fund it and justify that funding very eloquently.

If we had 900 high-powered florists in the Pentagon, you can bet they'd come up with reasons to spend, and waste, billions on flowers, rather than war. "Flowers are internationally understood as a symbol of beauty, peace, and prosperity. They are a natural mood enhancer, clinically more effective than Prozac," would be some likely diabolical horticulture propaganda. If 900 over-educated, puffy-chested English professors were driving our budget, be assured they would make a convincing case for comprehensive and expensive reading programs for the entire

61

nation. "Literacy and effective communication are the backbone of an advanced society," and other dogma, albeit true, would be inculcated into our brains by various strains of media.

And the flipside of this overbuilt war machine is that lately it is confoundingly ineffective. We have the most powerful, effective, well-trained military in the history of the world; in the 1940s we simultaneously defeated three of the world's most powerful militaries – Germany, Japan, and Italy – in a span of four years. Yet we have been fighting in Afghanistan, a country with no army, no navy, and no air force, for ten years without any clearly reported accomplishments (5). At a cost of somewhere between one and two trillion dollars, we were at war in tiny Iraq for as long as our involvement in World Wars I and II *combined*. How is this possible? It calls to mind the words of George Orwell who is credited with writing that "…war is not meant to be won; it is meant to be continuous." I cannot shake the feeling that our proud, honorable soldiers are essentially in these countries as a very elaborate and costly distraction while we take what we are really there for – oil and resources.

It is now rarely challenged that we are in Iraq principally for oil. In the case of Afghanistan, it leads the world in heroin production, and for years we've wanted to build an oil pipeline through the country from the Caspian Sea but the pesky Taliban controlled the country and wasn't amenable to that plan. We've also made some recent discoveries of enormous mineral deposits, which will cement our presence there for decades. Collectively, these are plenty of motives for invasion.

The 2007 documentary "No End in Sight" chronicles how in the chaotic wake of the U.S. invasion of Iraq, U.S. troops were not ordered to maintain civil order or to protect precious institutions such as government buildings, infrastructure, and treasured museums housing Babylonian artifacts. 15,000 artifacts were stolen from the National Museum of Iraq, for example. The country was literally descending into anarchy and the majority of our soldiers were immediately deployed to guard the oil fields. Several of my college students were Marines who served in Iraq and they corroborated that fact for me many times.

If we are in Iraq to free a people from tyranny and oppression, then why have we not protected the 400,000 who were slaughtered in Darfur or the 800,000 Rwandans that were killed by machete in the 90s? Why not protect southern Africans from the likes of Mobutu and Kabila in the DRC or from Mugabe's homicidal despotism in Zimbabwe? Could we not have stopped Pol Pot from rounding up and murdering one million of his Cambodian countrymen and women in the 1970s? I could go on.

One painful irony about the Iraq war is that Americans have now lost more lives in Iraq than we lost in 9/11. That statistic supports the idea that our greatest enemy may not be terrorists, but greed and self-initiated wars. Another oft-overlooked statistic about that war is that besides losing nearly 5,000 US service people, according to the Associated Press we have killed well over 100,000 Iraqis. That is thirty times as many people that died in 9/11. Have Iraqis perhaps received enough retribution? And besides, was Iraq ever officially connected in any way to the 9/11 bombings? It appears as though our proud armed forces have been used to beat up on someone and claim their oil – and the abused were never proven to have wronged us in the first place.

63

The attractive resources that Afghanistan possesses are not as widely known or publicized. While we were still picking through the rubble of the fallen Twin Towers, U.S. diplomats were meeting with the Pakistani oil minister about our desire to pipe oil through Afghanistan and out to Pakistani seaports. Meanwhile the newly-instated President Karzai was given $50 million by the Pentagon and $100 million by the IMF to build an oil-pipeline maintenance road.

An even more lucrative reason for being in Afghanistan surfaced in 2010, when Pentagon officials accompanied by U.S. geologists discovered huge veins of iron, copper, gold and valuable industrial metals like lithium worth an estimated $1 trillion (6). There are enough mineral deposits in the country to turn it into one of the world's leading mining centers. Based on this, I predict we will find reasons to stay in Afghanistan indefinitely.

But what interests me most is the U.S. government's fascination with illegal drugs. Our military has a very strong presence in the two largest drug producing regions on Earth – Colombia and Afghanistan – and it increasingly participates in the drug trafficking situation in Mexico. I personally became aware of the enormity of the drug industry while I was backpacking through South America in 1996.

Somehow I had ended up in an Ecuadorian military installation less than 100 miles from the Colombian border, being interrogated as a suspected drug smuggler. An apparently high-ranking Ecuadorian military officer began drilling me with questions in Spanish. My mind was reeling as I sat in the middle of a dark room with a light pointed at my face.

"¿Cuando llegaste a este país?" (When did you arrive in this country?)

"¿Y tu pasaporte, por qué no está estampado? (And why isn't your passport stamped?)

I did my best to answer the questions, but an accidental double-vaccination for yellow fever a month prior had basically induced the symptoms of yellow fever and it was blurring my memory along with other mental faculties. This only exacerbated the fact that my story, though truthful, sounded very fabricated. I had walked from northern Peru into Ecuador, so I never passed through an official customs station.

"¿Hace cuánto tiempo que estás en Ecuador? (How long have you been in Ecuador?)

I was trying to sound credible as the officer paced in circles around me, but it was clear that he thought I had purchased drugs in Colombia, crossed the border illegally, and was trying to utilize Quito airport's less stringent security as a way of getting off of the continent. So there I sat, pleading my case for freedom in my second language, with no way to contact another soul who could help me, fighting the symptoms of yellow fever, and not knowing what would possibly happen next.

I suppose that something in my eyes or the tone of my voice or body language finally gave him confidence in my story because my interrogator suddenly stopped pacing and said that they would stamp my passport and allow me to leave the country. But first, I would pay a "very big fine." I wildly imagined what the fine could be for suspected drug smuggling. In the end I gladly paid the fine of 1,000 Ecuadorian Sucres, which amounted to about U.S. $3.30.

I had gotten lucky, but I didn't realize at the time how extensive, pervasive, and multi-lateral the drug wars are in South America, Mexico, and Afghanistan. Nor did I understand how intimately involved the United States is on all levels of the industry.

The South American drug war has received much attention in the past three decades because it involves the flow of billions of dollars, principally between the U.S. and Colombia. Increasingly of late, the transport of these drugs into the U.S. has led to a dramatic increase in drug-cartel violence throughout Mexico and along the U.S./Mexico border. Moreover, Afghanistan's position as the world's largest producer of heroin has drawn hundreds of millions of dollars of attention from the United States government. Overall, the UN estimates that selling drugs in the United States, the world's largest drug consumer, amounts to $142 billion in annual business (7).

The prototype for U.S. involvement with a drug-production zone exists in the past three decades in Colombia, Peru, and Bolivia. The tactics that we have employed there are being played out now in both Mexico and Afghanistan. The United States government has entered this South American arena through substantial financial and military involvement, and following its strategies is both fascinating and bewildering. It is surprisingly difficult to determine what's going on below the surface of rhetoric, distraction, and shifting alliances in this hotbed of money and multi-directional conflict.

The stated goals of the United States in the drug war in South America have been to cultivate democracy, support human rights, and curb the production of cocaine and other drugs at the source. Its principal method of achieving these goals, has been the militarization of Latin America through what are called U.S. Security Assistance Programs. These programs include four basic elements: direct monetary funding for national militaries, supply of military technology and equipment, training by the U.S. armed forces, and strategic advice from the United States government.

Huh? Immediately there is a big contradiction between the humanitarian, benevolent goals of the government, and the aggressive, militarily-focused approach that is actually being employed. Sometimes it's more fruitful to look at the tangible results of such an intervention rather than trying to sift through rhetoric for some solid truth.

Taking this approach, there are four main outcomes that are consistently seen as a result of the U.S. Security Assistance Programs. First, countries in the region are destabilized because the fortified militaries surpass the power of national governments. There are frequent assassinations of anti-drug politicians, and martial (military) law is often imposed in times of "emergency." This chronology in the country of Colombia, the center of the drug trade, shows a strong correlation between U.S. involvement, militarization, and the promotion of the drug trade:

In 1982, President Belisario Betancur is elected, and in 1983 he rejects the U.S. supported extradition treaty (to oust drug czars from the country). In following, the U.S. imposes heavy economic sanctions on Colombia – mainly flowers, perishable goods, and the airlines were affected (8). In 1984, in response to guerilla activity, the Colombian legislature deems the country to be in a state of siege, which greatly expands military and police power (reminiscent of the post 9/11 Patriot Act) (9). In the same year, Justice Minister and outspoken anti-drug critic, Rodrigo Lara, is assassinated. Five years later in 1989, Luis Carlos Galan, anti-drug presidential candidate is assassinated. The newly elected president institutes the extradition policy desired by the U.S., militarization of the drug war increases substantially, and the president signs the Decree Law of 1989, "which empowered armed forces to arrest and hold suspects incommunicado for up to seven days in military installations"(10).

Due to the U.S.'s heightened control and influence in the country, one thing is quite clear; it is very dangerous for any member of the Colombian government to be openly against the drug trade or to openly counter any suggestion from the U.S. government.

The second observable result of U.S. involvement is the prevalence of human rights abuses. Specifically, U.S.-trained Latin American military are consistently high human rights abusers. In the words of Jimmy Carter, "The outcome of such training has made Latin American military less humane, less professional, and increasingly focused on civilian (non-military) affairs" (11). In Mexico and Bolivia, the areas where U.S.-sponsored local military anti-drug efforts are greatest, reported human-rights violations are also at their highest.

U.S. presence also generates indiscriminate military expansion and activity, often irrespective of any specific or clear goal. The Colombian government was supplied with twelve Cobra helicopters by the U.S. military, and in the words of author Eugene Bouley, Jr., "the bottom line is that the law permits the use of such weapons only for counter-narcotics operations, but increasingly U.S. representatives, both military and civilian, nod and wink when weapons are used against guerillas and other civilians" (12). In addition, in attempts to fight leftist guerillas, U.S.-sponsored militaries often join with drug-cartel paramilitary groups in attacking and opposing guerillas. This barrage of military activity can make it extremely difficult to determine actual motives, real progress, and actions, which are truly effective. It seems as though hyper-active military presence itself is one of the goals.

The fourth result of U.S. involvement is that there has been a steady *increase* in the supply of drugs since the early 1980s, when our presence in Colombia began in earnest. This is ascertainable through CIA and UN estimates of how much money is flowing back to Colombia from the U.S. on an annual basis, which has been fairly consistent or expanding in the past two decades. Further evidence of increased supply is the decrease in the price of cocaine, specifically from $55,000 per kilo in 1980 to $10,500 per kilo in 1995 (13). This is also the case in Afghanistan. President Karzai and the U.S. Defense Department have repeatedly resisted supporting anti-drug actions in Afghanistan (14). In fact, in 2006, five years after initial U.S. military involvement in the country, the total acreage of poppy fields cultivated (the raw material for opium and heroin production) was 165,000 hectares, the largest heroin crop in Afghan history (15). Due to expansion in the southern part of the country, the national crop was even larger in 2007.

In looking at the tangible evidence, there begins to be a clear connection between U.S. involvement and the *promotion,* not the inhibition of the drug trade. These results do not match on any level with the stated goals of the U.S. in this intervention in Latin America. If the casual observer inputs new goals, which seem to match more logically with the observable results of our presence in the region, the scene can take on a new clarity. The first of what could be called our "true goals" in Latin America has been to create chaos, destabilization, and war. This creates fear, legitimizes military aggression, and creates a willingness by civilians and government to surrender freedoms in the name of greater perceived safety through heightened military presence. This, as stated above, is precisely what happened inside the borders of the U.S. with the post 9/11 Patriot Act, the quintessence of "Big Brother" vigilance.

The second true goal is expansion of the military and military activity. This desensitizes the public to the military, gives those in control access to valuable natural resources (drugs or oil), and lets the military monitor money flow in the country. The Afghan national army, for instance, was trained by U.S. military. The Pentagon has also promised to supply the U.S. Drug Enforcement Agency operating in Afghanistan with Mi-17 helicopters but has been slow to deliver (16). Perhaps the DEA's more aggressive drug enforcement approach does not jibe with the Pentagon's larger goals in the area. Also, by 1996, 1,000 Mexican police officers had received special counter-narcotics training in the United States (17).

A third true goal has been the ideological separation between military and the democratic governmental process. This is achieved by keeping a country in a constant state of "emergency" and fear of imminent attack, so that rational constitutional legalities vanish. The military is granted total license to abuse civil and human rights or the environment in order to bring about greater safety. A high level of fear, especially of being attacked or killed by an unseen yet publicly identified force, puts individuals in a primal survival state in which the foundation of a legal, humane society (a constitution or general moral code) is essentially ineffectual. In other words, the population is placed in a state of "no holds barred" and "anything goes" because of their extreme fear. And this is an ideal situation for any military wishing to have access to and control over various societal and economic endeavors.

The fourth mechanism of U.S. intervention is to disguise its motives with a façade of words and actions. This is such a common mechanism of political machines in general, but a few U.S. administrations have employed this more than others. In each case our apparent magnanimity is just a crime, renamed. "Fighting terrorism" = Justifying an invasion. "Drug War" = Drug cultivation. "Bring them to justice" = Assassinate non-supporters. "Peace-keeping missiles" = Bombs that kill thousands of people.

Fifth is our failure by design. We purposely fail at our stated goal of stopping or diminishing the drug trade, because this allows us to prolong our presence in the region in order to pursue our true goals, which are to cultivate and profit from the drug trade. If it is not by design, then it is quite curious that the most powerful military in the world cannot topple some peasant coca bean farmers and drug gangs with semi-automatic rifles. If we wanted the South American drug war to be over, it would have been so long ago. Similarly, amidst ongoing war in Afghanistan, schools, synagogues, and public services have suffered greatly, yet drug production is thriving. It is widely known that heroin production finances both the Taliban as well as President Karzai's administration, so it is no wonder that drug eradication is proving slow and difficult.

Lastly, America's most sought-after true goal has been to maintain sovereignty over the flow of money in this industry. We do so by constantly shifting our loyalties and alliances in order to take down any powerful individuals or groups in the industry and take over their portion of commerce. We skillfully play government officials and drug czars off each other in order to accomplish this. The U.S. ousts drug czars with the help of government extradition policies, and at the same time condones the assassination of uncooperative politicians with the help of drug czars. This shifting of alliances has been very commonly utilized by our government for decades in myriad global situations. One minute a politician or drug leader is our friend, the next they are our hunted foe. Saddam had helped the CIA overthrow the Iraqi leadership in the 60s, while Bin Laden was supported by the CIA in his efforts against the Soviet invasion of Afghanistan. Other former U.S. bed buddies who have since fallen out of favor are Manuel Noriega and Joseph Mobutu of Zaire.

There is much evidence showing how the Taliban was supported in the late 90s by the CIA. In his book *Descent into Chaos*, Pakistani journalist Ahmed Rashid states, "Between 1995 and 1996, the USA supported the Taliban politically through its allies in Pakistan and Saudi Arabia, essentially because Washington viewed the Taliban as anti-Iranian, anti-Shia, and pro-Western" (18). British journalist Simon Reeves supports claims that the U.S. supplied Taliban forces with arms and satellite imagery, while author Robert Dreyfuss claims that "U.S. diplomats saw them (the Taliban) as messianic do-gooders – like born again Christians from the American Bible belt" (19). Needless to say, the Taliban has fallen from our good graces in the U.S. and is now perceived as public enemy number one.

After analysis of these true goals, what is occurring, yet rarely publicized, in drug-producing nations seems very logical: drug income in Colombia has been stabilized and the supply of cocaine has increased, US military presence in Latin America and Afghanistan has been amply secured, and poppy cultivation in Afghanistan has increased dramatically since initial U.S. invasion in 2001 (20).

The U.S. military's strength has righted many wrongs and brought widespread stability in some critical moments in the past 150 years of global history. My father and his brothers played a part in that honorable quest. In the past few decades, however, it seems as though our goal has been to expand the military indiscriminately in order to achieve a range of goals, some noble and some otherwise. The motives for our recent military involvement in Iraq, Afghanistan, and Colombia are often questioned, and these wars have drained our national coffers in the process. Our current economic recession is forcing us to scrutinize our spending habits as a nation. Hopefully, it will precipitate the call for an end to these questionable wars and a return to a focus on real human issues and institutions here at home that so badly need our attention.

Returning to Organic Food

"The Lord God took the man and put him in the Garden of Eden to till it and keep it."

- Genesis 2:15

The First Way to Save the Planet: Eat Organic

It heals our bodies and our soils. Organic food does not contain the pesticides and synthetic fertilizers that contribute to high cancer rates in industrialized countries, nor does it contain the high fructose corn syrup or trans-fatty acids that are leading to obesity and diabetes. The prevalence of these diseases is overwhelming our health care system. And antioxidants in organic food slow the aging process. A significant increase in consumption of organic food would save billions of dollars in reduced health care costs every year. Moreover, going organic heals our soils all over the planet that have been depleted and polluted by over-farming and excessive chemicals for decades. Organic farmers rotate crops, rest the soil after a few growing seasons, and do not add synthetic chemicals, all of which restores health and productivity to the soil exactly when we need it most – to feed our planet's exploding population. Sustainability is the key because soil is essentially a non-renewable resource.

I had never seen food this beautiful before. Cherries, pears, arugula, mushrooms, and a lush abundance of other fruits and vegetables adorned the racks as I stood in the back cooler at *Chez Panisse* in Berkeley, California – one of America's first all-organic, gourmet restaurants. I had earned a one-day tryout in which I would prepare the morel mushroom pasta sauce for the vegetarian menu option that evening at this famous prix-fixe establishment. The head chef and other senior chefs gathered at a table and, as was clearly customary, discussed what freshly-delivered ingredients would be included in the evening's supper. All the while, this clergy of food epicureans were methodically snapping open fava beans to save precious prep time for one of the day's appetizers. The care and skill that the team of renowned chefs displayed when discussing and preparing food was both impressive and endearing to me.

All day long my senses were delighted as crate after crate of vibrant, fragrant, organic produce, often picked that very day, was being delivered to the restaurant. The restaurant's trend-setting fame is a testament to the foresight of its owner and vehement "locavore," Alice Waters.

My tryout was a success, and I was offered a job, but I ended up finding a better permanent fit as manager of a nearby raw and organic café called *Raw Energy*. *Chez Panisse* and *Raw Energy* are still in existence and thriving, and my experience at both locations fortified my love of healthy organic food which has only increased in the decade following. It always struck me how physically different my clientele at *Raw Energy* looked compared to the customers at, say, a fast food restaurant, or even a mainstream grocery store. If the skin, eyes, and energy level of my clients were any testament, there is definitely something different, and better for us, about eating organic food.

There are three very compelling reasons why we should shift to eating more organic food. First, eating organic food slows the aging process as well as the development of cancer. Second, it will save us billions of dollars in healthcare costs every year, and third it heals our plant's depleted and polluted soils.

For 10,000 years, all agriculture practiced on Earth was organic and natural. Only in the past century, in an effort to keep up with the skyrocketing global population, "conventional agriculture" emerged which employed heavy chemical inputs and genetically modified crops in order to increase yields. This industrial agriculture approach did grow more food, which saved lives, but its downside has been a heavy price to pay. All conventional crops are sprayed with deadly insecticides and herbicides which are proven to cause cancer in humans, and a large proportion of these crops are genetically modified.

What's crazy is that the USDA does not require that these deadly chemicals and genetic changes be labeled. Profit-driven conventional farming also drains soil of its nutrients by never allowing it to rest and be replenished, while toxifying the soil with chemical pesticides and fertilizers. In other words, just as a rise in population rates is generating more mouths to feed, our soils are slowly being destroyed by our agricultural status quo.

I personally began eating organic food about ten years ago, and my diet has varied from 50% - 95% organic over the years. I have noticed several changes in my body, some significant and some subtle. First, I am undeniably leaner. Chemicals on food which are unidentifiable to the body are often stored in fatty tissues. When I cleansed my body by simply ingesting fewer and fewer chemicals, I also shed some fat in the process. In addition, I noticed that eating organic fruits and vegetables gave my skin better protection from the sun and improved the appearance of my skin in general. In fact, about three months after I began drinking fresh organic juices, people began to comment that my skin looked healthier. Overall, my physical endurance increased, my system just felt cleaner, and I seemed to wake up feeling more refreshed as a result of eating more organic food.

In the past few decades, organic agriculture has blossomed into a $40 billion industry world-wide, largely in response to the drawbacks of conventional farming (1). So then, what exactly *is* organic farming? Very simply, organic farmers do *not* use chemical fertilizers, chemical pesticides, or genetically modified or engineered seeds. What organic farmers *do* utilize is growing a wide variety of crops, rotating crops, using only natural fertilizers (manure or compost), and always leaving a section of the land in fallow, or rest, so that it may fully recover before being planted again (2). A fallow period helps humus, or living matter, to develop in the soil, keeping soil moist, fertile, and life-giving. These are some of the reasons why organic food has more vitamins, minerals, and anti-oxidants than food grown with chemicals on over-farmed soils (3)(4)(5).

The abundant antioxidants in organic food literally slow down the aging process, because antioxidants neutralize the free radicals that cause cell damage and also lead to cancer. Some general sources of these harmful free radicals are smoking, a diet high in meat, fat, and sugar, too much sun, as well as toxic chemicals *and* toxic emotions. Eating organic fruits, veggies, nuts, and grains is nature's built-in way of neutralizing the free radicals in our environment and slowing the aging process in our bodies. But we tamper with this beautifully balanced system when we as a society spray our crops with toxic pesticides repeatedly throughout the growing cycle. Perhaps this is why, despite our superior health care in the West, our cancer incidence rates are approximately double that of the developing world.

Walking around on an organic farm is a delight to the senses, and you can reach down, pick, and eat anything that may catch your eye. This is not the case on conventional farms which are laced with chemical pesticides, and I wouldn't suggest picking and eating anything before you give it a pretty serious scrubbing with soap and a brush.

"Given that most Americans eat conventionally-produced food," states one pro-organic author, "the diminished vitamin and mineral content of this food could lead to long-term nutritional inferiority and adverse health effects" (6). Countless studies have proven the nutritional superiority of eating organic. In a study that investigated forty-one previous nutritional studies published in the *Journal of Alternative and Complimentary Medicine,* organic crops were shown to contain substantially more vitamin C, iron, magnesium, phosphorous, and usable protein than conventional crops (7)(8). Specific organic crops such as strawberries, blackberries, and corn have been shown to contain more antioxidants than their conventional counterparts (9). And a study done in the U.S. divulged that people who have eaten an organic diet have more antioxidants in their systems (10). That food has healing properties is not a new concept. Over two thousand years ago, Hippocrates, the father of Western medicine himself, wrote "Let food be thy medicine."

So, who's growing organic food? Australia actually has more organic cropland than any other country, but organic farming has its strongest regional foothold in Europe – comprising at least 10% of farms in Denmark, Austria, and Switzerland – and it's also now found in 90 developing countries on a commercial scale (11). The entire nation of Cuba went from Soviet-subsidized conventional farming to 100% organic food production in the span of only a few years. In the U.S. organic farming still only accounts for less than two percent of the total agricultural output, but exploding consumer demand for organic food is changing that landscape rapidly (12).

As a geography professor, I find an organic farm to be the perfect environment in which to teach students how humans and the Earth work together in symbiosis. For several semesters I have brought about 100 of my students to Tierra Miguel organic farm to plant, harvest, and taste everything from butter lettuce and carrots to cherry tomatoes and strawberries. About thirty minutes removed from the main highway in the Pauma Valley of southern California, the only sounds audible on the 87-acre farm are the rustling of horses at a nearby stable, the occasional cry of a red-tailed hawk, and the wind itself.

The knowing, healing timbre in the voices of the farm's owners, Mil and Leia Krecu, is alone worth the trip. A few students initially balk at the physical labor or the "dirt everywhere," but by the end of the day, I always witness a transformation, and many don't want to leave. Every vegetable grown on the farm is crisp and light. The strawberries are by far the best that I've ever tasted. And according to my students, once someone tastes food like this, they'll be hooked for life. Experience leads me to agree.

Chemical-intensive conventional farms are quite different. Spanning thousands of acres in the U.S. Midwest, a typical conventional farm will grow genetically modified corn and soy beans while hired pilots fly overhead dousing the fields with deadly insecticides. Anonymous workers drive massive combines which harvest the "product" with stunning speed and efficiency. Then trucks ship the chemical-laden, genetically-tampered foods to our supermarket shelves, where, without labels, they seem perfectly healthy and nutritious. Pointing to conventional farming's impersonal process and unilateral focus on higher profits, author Wendell Berry comments that "the economy of money has infiltrated and subverted the economies of nature, energy, and the human spirit." (13).

This brings up perhaps the most harmful aspect of agri-business: the fact that 2-20 pounds per acre of insecticides and herbicides (collectively called "pesticides") are sprayed on fields during each growing season, depending on the crop. These toxins reside in the soil and wash into streams and groundwater supplies. In fact, the modern environmental movement is often said to have begun with the 1962 publication of Rachel Carson's *Silent Spring*, which was an outcry against rampant pesticide use. In all there are hundreds of pesticides being used in the U.S. at any given time.

Each year a large number of these pesticides are proven to be carcinogenic and hence made illegal. But chemical companies like Dow, Dupont, Bayer, and Monsanto simply instruct their chemists to invent new pesticides, which will then proliferate for at least ten years before sufficient research can again prove them to be cancer-causing and illegal. This cat-and-mouse game has gone on for decades. When huge inventories of a particular pesticide are deemed illegal, their producers just sell them to developing-world nations where these restrictions are non-existent or unenforced.

Another glaring negative of conventional farms, which currently make up 99% of U.S. farms and a majority of farms in the developed world, is that they use harmful synthetic fertilizers. Made from fossil fuels, synthetic fertilizers systematically kill good bacteria, the life-force of the soil. Topsoil becomes dry and lifeless and essentially turns to dust. Bringing to mind scenes from *The Grapes of Wrath*, China's Changjiang valley has turned into a dust bowl and 2.4 billion tons of topsoil have been blown or washed away (14). In the U.S. south, after a century of heavy pesticide application on top of 300 years of intensive tobacco and cotton cultivation on already poor "ultisol" terrain, the soils are now among the most depleted on planet Earth.

Let's delve a little further into why organic foods have more vitamins, minerals, and antioxidants than conventional crops. It seems clear that there are some intangible elements at play. For example, in a commonly replicated test, people who eat homemade chicken soup as opposed to canned chicken soup recover faster from the influenza virus, a.k.a. the common cold. Is it the human care and love that goes into the home-cooked meal that speeds recovery? I became aware of a very similar effect with organic food when I managed *Raw Energy* organic café and came to know several of my organic farmer suppliers. I would hear them talking about their farm or soil as if it were a loved one: "Yeah, she's beautiful. I've been spending a lot of time with her lately and she's recovered well. She's ready. I mean, just look at these cabbages!"

The food from those farmers almost seemed to glow with their love. I felt good about serving it to my customers. Could that love possibly be the cause of the higher antioxidant counts and more vitamins and minerals in organic foods? It's difficult to prove scientifically, but in my opinion, it is absolutely possible.

The poorest of the poor normally don't have a choice of whether to eat organic or conventional food. For the past thirty years, the World Food Program has had the tall order of finding ways to feed the world's most destitute populations. Increasing the amount of food produced per acre of land was seen as the necessary end, and genetic modification of seeds was viewed as the means to get there. Huge amounts of financing in the 1980s, and more recently from Bill Gates, has gone into the development of genetically modified organisms, or GMOs.

GMOs are seeds that are genetically altered by splicing in DNA from other plants and even animals in order to give the resultant plant certain desirable traits, such as resistance to specific pests, more resilience during drought or frost, or even just to make a fruit bigger or sweeter. For example, genes from a salmon may be inserted into a corn plant, or genes from a sweet potato may be spliced into a fruit tree. Countless nations across the globe will not purchase GMO crops because they are wary of the possible negative effects. Yet, not only is the U.S. the largest consumer of genetically modified organisms, the USDA does not even require that they be labeled.

The result is that in the United States, GMO crops abound with 72% of all GMO crops on Earth being grown in this country. In fact, about 85% of corn, 90% of cotton, and 95% of soybeans in the U.S. are GMO crops (15). These modified seed crops do produce higher yields, but we have no idea what effect these gene-spliced organisms are having on human beings. In the words of author Leslie Duram:

"With no long-term safety studies, we've introduced these new genetically-altered materials to our environment and into our bodies. We simply do not have the facts on GMOs, yet we are currently conducting a massive experiment on you, me, the rest of society, and our ecosystems. Organic agriculture and buying organic food are the only way to avoid being part of this global experiment...(which is) being driven by the profit motives of several agribusiness and pharmaceutical corporations" (16).

Many of these biotech firms are substantial contributors to political campaigns, which may explain the passing of the 1996 Freedom to Farm Act whereby agribusiness companies and conventional farmers are now given $20 to $25 billion in annual subsidies from American tax payers. Beyond lobbying for government handouts, the principal way that biotech companies make money is to "patent nature." That is, these companies are allowed to artificially generate a biological product, patent it, and thereby have exclusive rights to sell it. One cannot patent apples or corn as they occur in nature, so laboratory-produced versions of them are generated, advertised as superior, patented, and then sold. Biotech firms even spend millions on advertising which puts a positive "emotional" spin on genetically engineered foods (17).

What's more, farmers are forced to sign contracts with major GMO corporations, such as Monsanto, that state they will only use their brand of pesticides and that they will not use the seeds bought one year on the next year's crop. Some farmers are even sued because they are caught allegedly growing GMO crops without a contract, like the infamous case against Indiana farmer David Runyon. This industry has gone so far as to produce "suicidal genes," which cause a seed to self-destruct after several months, ensuring that it can only be used for a given year's planting (18).

The largest producers of GMO seeds in the world are Monsanto, DuPont, and Syngenta. The most prominent of the three, Monsanto, began as a chemical company producing DDT and Agent Orange during the Vietnam War era. The company's genetic engineering of seeds began so they could modify and sell a soybean that was tolerant of its most profitable herbicide, called "Roundup." In 1996, two percent of U.S. soybeans contained the Monsanto "Roundup-ready" gene, but by 2008, over ninety percent of all soybeans in the U.S. contained the gene (19).

On a positive note, the GMO movement has increased yields on innumerable farms around the world (thanks largely to genetic engineering "founding father" Norman Borlaug), and many GMO scientists have earnestly magnanimous goals that their food-engineering feats will feed the planet. Their efforts have, indeed, staved off starvation for millions of people for a few decades. That is a victory by any account. Yet this victory is necessarily short-lived, as the heavy chemicals applied to fields in order to produce these yields have so polluted and depleted soils as often to render them essentially infertile.

Further marring the GMO victory party is that its seeds and chemical inputs are very expensive, so the process instantly puts farmers into debt-dependency to biotech companies. There is a growing consensus that genetic engineering is simply another way for huge corporations to reap profits at the expense of the environment and the less fortunate. For example, U.S. efforts at rebuilding Afghanistan have included importing pesticide, fertilizer, and GMO companies to educate and supply local farmers. But this is completely incongruous with local agricultural and social tradition, not to mention wildly expensive for such an impoverished rural population.

Dr. Tewolde, general manager of Ethiopia's Environmental Protection Authority, wrote that "GE (genetic engineering) threatens to make the problem (food insecurity) worse, creating dependence on corporate-owned agricultural inputs such as seed, decreasing the need for labor, decreasing agricultural diversity, promoting agribusiness over family farms… (etc.)" (20).

In early 20th century Europe, like today, organic agriculture struggled to survive against the powerful chemical companies. This conflict was expressed most vividly when the "bio-dynamic" agricultural movement was banned by the Nazis beginning in 1940 due to pressure exerted upon them by the German chemical companies (21). The German government of that era was focused on generating the largest agricultural output possible in order to sustain economic and wartime prosperity, with the environment being essentially ignored (22). Soon, observations of the deleterious effects of such agriculture were commonplace, which coupled with an expanded demand for healthier foods to spur a resurgence of natural food cultivation in Europe. A very similar transition to healthier agricultural practices is happening right now in the United States, despite heavy and continued legislative support of chemical agribusiness techniques.

For the consumer who is wondering, "Where can I buy organic food near me?" the answer is at your local farmer's market, Trader Joe's or Whole Foods markets. Markets in your local region offering organic foods are mentioned in the "Practical Suggestions" chapter of this book. You can also become part of a CSA (Community Supported Agriculture) in which you pay a local organic farm around $25 - $30 every two weeks to deliver to you a large box full of whatever has been freshly picked on the farm.

In conclusion, it's now apparent that more focus on organic, sustainable cultivation is an inevitable future for global agriculture. An encouraging sign was that by the year 2000, more organic food was sold in mainstream supermarkets than in natural-food stores, marking its shift into mainstream consumption. Also, thanks to the efforts of First Lady Michelle Obama, the White House front lawn was graced by an organic garden. As farmers and food shoppers increasingly acquiesce to the overwhelming environmental, economic, and health benefits of organic foods, a profound shift is occurring in the way that we grow and consume food on this planet. Hopefully this transition will involve less resistance from agri-business giants and more conscientious decision-making on the part of industry and government leaders as well as consumers who recognize the huge personal and collective advantages of going organic.

The Miracle of Solar Power

"We are like tenant farmers chopping down the fence around our house for fuel when we should be using Nature's inexhaustible sources of energy -- sun, wind and tide. ... I'd put my money on the sun and solar energy. What a source of power! I hope we don't have to wait until oil and coal run out before we tackle that."

-Thomas Edison, inventor (1847-1931)

"The ice caps wouldn't be melting, and neither would I...energy would fall right down from the sky... that's my dream world."

**-"Dreamworld" (2009) by Robin Thicke,
Grammy Award-Winning R&B Singer**

"Solar power is the biggest business opportunity the world has ever seen."

**- Ted Turner, billionaire, philanthropist and creator
of CNN, the first 24 hour news network (1)**

The Second Way to Save the Planet: Convert to Solar

Solar power is inexpensive, ubiquitous, produces no pollution, and it never runs out. In the next fifty years, it will transform the global economy, the environment, and it will dramatically enhance U.S. national security. Adoption of solar power and other renewables, such as wind power, on a large scale means replacing coal as the main producer of our electricity. This saves millions of tons of CO2 from going into our atmosphere every year. This shift in energy sources, along with reducing meat consumption, are the two most effective ways to diminish global warming that the industrialized world can make. A change to renewable energy will also translate to drastically reduced dependence on foreign sources of energy, such as oil. This means less money spent on wars and military activity, and therefore less provoking of terrorist retaliation. Most solar companies now provide and install solar panels for free, through what is called the solar lease program. You can also vote for solar power to be implemented in your city, state, and your nation.

While I'm cozy on the couch watching the National Geographic channel on my new plasma TV, somewhere far, far away in a coal-fired electricity plant, one pound of carbon dioxide is being spewed into the air in order to power my television for one hour. If I were running my central air conditioning unit for that same hour, another six pounds of CO_2 would be released into our blue American skies (2). In fact, 65% of the electricity produced in America is made from burning fossil fuels, principally coal, while another 20% comes from nuclear power. It almost seems like there aren't any feasible alternatives.

Interesting, then, isn't it that there are entire communities in Germany that are 100% solar-powered, and large solar power plants have been functional elsewhere for over a century? What's more, solar panels are now installed on U.S. homes by most major companies for free, yes **for free**, and then provide cheap electricity for the life of the home and never produce one speck of CO_2. Imagine running the AC unit all-day-long without the guilt...or the cost.

So, given this, why didn't this country, let alone the entire world, convert to solar power long ago? Indeed, that is the $250 billion question. Why that amount? Far from random, $250 billion was the gross profit racked up last year by selling electricity that was generated from the burning of fossil fuels in this country (3). That amount of cash is a pretty good incentive for coal and natural gas suppliers to suppress and denounce the obviously superior competitor of solar power. If I owned a coal-fired electricity plant, I would be absolutely terrified at the prospect of a much cheaper, zero-emission energy source that literally falls down from the sky. How can you compete with sunshine?

The benefits of solar energy are so grand that they are difficult to absorb: zero emissions, unlimited supply, available virtually everywhere, and after the one-time cost of building a solar power facility, free energy simply rains down… forever. There will be no need to create wars in order to steal another nation's energy. "Give me all your sunshine – or else," doesn't have much of a ring to it. Also, the negatives of fossil fuels, including perpetual war, billions of tons of annual air pollution, millions of gallons of oil spilled regularly, and scarring enormous tracts of land in order to dig for coal or natural gas will no longer be necessary. This grand vision won't happen immediately, but solar power, along with other renewables, are the way to get there.

The list of reasons why the United States has not largely espoused solar power ranges from censorship to sabotage to – and likely the most damning of all – a simple lack of public familiarity with this world-changing but simple technology. While awareness of solar energy is now exploding, it still faces an uphill fight against the powers-that-be. Yet as the Earth's consumption of energy escalates by nearly 40% in the next twenty years, causing an unwieldy rise in electricity costs, solar homes will be producing their own energy right at home: off the grid, emission-free and independent of any market or government agency. On the political spectrum, that's the Democratic *and* the Republican ideal all in one (4).

Few people realize that homeowners can now switch to clean solar power for free. Most U.S. solar companies now offer a "solar lease" in which they install photovoltaic solar panels on your home for zero money down, and payments are usually crafted to be smaller than the household's current monthly electricity bill. So nearly everyone can go solar and instantly *save* money! Solar City is the largest residential supplier of solar power in the U.S., and currently operates in 20 states. This company is one of several which are making the dream of a solar-powered world into a reality.

The world needs a lot of energy in order to function each day. We need fuel for our cars, power for our factories, and electricity to light and heat our homes and to charge all of our gadgets. If sun and wind were providing all of this energy, your daily routine would not change one bit, except that the air that you breathe and water that you drink wouldn't be polluted by fossil fuels.

Providing energy to the world, in the form of oil, made John D. Rockefeller III and J. Paul Getty two of the richest men the world has ever known. Oil money boosted both Bushes into the U.S. presidency and it was also, ironically, much of the foundation of the Bin Laden family's wealth and political power. In the 21st century, self-made billionaires will also provide energy for the world, but now that energy will come from the sun. As evidence of this, Shi Zhengrong, creator of Suntech, a solar cell manufacturer, is already China's second wealthiest man (5).

In the words of author Frank Kryza, "Harnessing the sun's energy is one of human kind's oldest fantasies, ranking with perpetual motion and the transmutation of base metals into gold" (6). The ancient Greek engineer Archimedes set fire to enemy ships with the reflected light of the sun, while Leonardo da Vinci proposed the idea of solar power being used for commercial purposes. In 1912, American engineer, Frank Shuman, built a solar plant in Egypt that pumped 6,000 gallons of Nile river water per minute onto nearby cotton fields. After Shuman's great success in Egypt, many thought solar energy was poised to make a big transition into popular usage (7).

Just before the outset of World War I in February of 1914, Shuman wrote in *Scientific American*: "Sun power is now a fact and no longer in the 'beautiful possibility' stage… (It will have) a history something like aerial navigation. The Wrights made an 'actual record' flight and thereafter developments were more rapid. We have made an 'actual record' in sun power and we also hope now for quick developments" (8).

Months later, those plans were dashed by the first World War as the hubbub and fervor of battle pulled our attention away from the miracle of solar power, and this amazing technological revolution went into dormancy. Today, war is used as a distraction as often as it is used for territorial or tactical gain, and the current political climate on the globe is tumultuous enough to again divert us from the simple, clean, bountiful gift of solar energy. But rapid changes in our environment are galvanizing us to make wiser energy choices.

For instance, utilizing our local sunshine to power our homes and cars makes us more self- sufficient as a nation. This means that we don't have to go to war overseas just to supply our energy needs. What if it required war to supply our high levels of dairy or sugar consumption? Would that be worth it? We must realize the inherent absurdity of waging war and killing thousands of people just to support our excessive lifestyle choices – especially when we have plenty of cheap, clean energy right here at home. Author Jennifer Carless suggests that since national security is such an issue of late, energy self-sufficiency should be our first goal, because then need for foreign military invasion would profoundly diminish (9).

Traipsing through rural Africa or Southeast Asia, once in a while you will encounter a small shack or even a mud hut with a single solar panel on its roof. I've seen entire villages crowded into one such hut to watch a soccer match on a television that was powered by the sun. One east African man who lived far removed from any sizeable town explained that his tiny solar panel was enough to power his television or phone charger or a coffee maker, but only one at a time. These cases highlight one of solar power's greatest assets: flexibility. It can be collected on a small enough scale to power a watch, a calculator, or a single family home, but also can be gleaned in enormous multi-megawatt centralized energy plants. No fossil-fuel energy source can make that claim.

That is important because two billion people worldwide are not connected to the electric power grid. They are ideal candidates for local solar energy collection, because building a coal or nuclear-powered energy plant then running power lines to the surrounding communities would be prohibitively costly. This is why countless solar energy projects are springing up in the developing world, mainly for water pumping and electric lighting (10). At of the time of publication of this book, globally solar power produces approximately 200 Gigawatts of energy at full capacity, which is enough to power all of Europe or all of Africa (approximately 750 million homes at European consumption rates) (11). Solar production is skyrocketing at approximately 25% annually (12) while coal, oil, and natural gas supplies are diminishing the world over. Moreover, the solar industry already provides more jobs than the oil extraction or coal industries (13).

Much of the debate over which energy source to use is more complicated than it needs to be. All that really happens in a coal-fired, natural gas-fired, or nuclear-powered energy plant is that the coal, gas, or uranium heats water until it boils and the steam is used to spin turbines which create electricity. The same exact process happens in a concentrated solar power (CSP) plant where hundreds of mirrors are positioned to reflect the sun's heat to a central tower, and that heat is used to boil water, turning turbines and producing electricity.

Why would a community or nation ever choose dirty coal or radioactive uranium over, of all things, sunshine in order to fuel the same exact energy-making process? Only old ideas, old habits, and greed of those who make money from selling fossil fuels and uranium can explain such a decision. And we must remember that we have the power to change this by voting for and purchasing energy from renewable sources. Ignorance and apathy are the best friends of those who profit from selling products that ruin our environment.

Just outside of Los Angeles, California, a massive 400-megawatt concentrated solar power (CSP) project by Bright Source Energy has just been completed which powers 140,000 homes and provides jobs for hundreds of workers (14). Southern California Edison has already signed a contract to pay Bright Source Energy $800 million *per year* for the electricity that they will be providing to the Los Angeles area. And here's the catch; their raw material – sunshine – is free. How's that for a business plan. In fact, the raw materials for all truly renewable energy sources are both free and infinite. Tough to argue that renewable energy isn't good for the economy with those stats staring back at you.

Each of the renewable energies, including wind, biomass, geothermal, wave, and solar power, are an improvement on fossil fuels, and they are all growing in prevalence every year. I personally see solar energy as having the best potential for

95

replacing fossil fuels on a mass scale, but I support and welcome all truly renewable sources of energy. For instance, Denmark currently taps a full 50% of its energy from the wind, and Iceland's extensive use of geothermal and hydroelectric energy will soon make it the globe's first society that is entirely free of fossil fuels (15). During his State of the Union address in January of 2010, President Obama stated, "The nation that leads the clean-energy economy is the nation that will lead the global economy. The United States must be that nation." By the year 2030, some estimates suggest that renewables could supply close to half of America's energy needs (16).

What about biomass energy? This involves producing ethanol and biodiesel from plants to be used as a cleaner-burning fuel in our cars. In essence, millions of acres of sugarcane in Brazil and millions of acres of corn in the U.S. end up feeding our cars each year, not our stomachs. This image highlights a big downside to this process: it competes with food for cropland which drives up food costs, and it also often involves deforestation. For these reasons, most biomass energy is not truly renewable nor is it sustainable on a mass scale. Ethanol made from rice husks and other agricultural or forestry waste products, however, doesn't have these side effects, nor does biodiesel made from algae or used cooking oil (17).

In the words of visionary billionaire businessman, Ted Turner, "Our future depends on changing the way we use energy. We've got to move away from fossil fuels and develop long-term energy solutions that work. Using clean energy technologies such as solar power is the right thing to do, and it represents a tremendous business opportunity" (18).

One concept that I always used to convey to my college students is that solar power and fossil fuels are both really just sunlight in different forms. Fossil fuels are dead plants and animals which have decayed and condensed over millions of years into fossilized form. Plants survive by converting the sun's energy into chemical energy through photosynthesis, and animals survive by consuming this stored energy in plants. Therefore, the "life force" in plant and animal remains, or fossil fuels, is simply ancient, degraded, condensed sunlight. So oil and coal are ancient sunlight stored in liquid or solid form. Solar energy is fresh, un-degraded and utilizable sunlight in its highest and purest energy form. The fact that using fresh solar energy generates essentially no negative effects on the environment, while burning decayed, old, fossilized solar energy (fossil fuels) pollutes the air, damages living things, and is causing the globe to heat up is a clear sign from nature guiding us to the best form of the sun's power.

In 2015, the approximate total amount of energy consumed worldwide from all sources was 110,000 terawatts (19). That same amount of energy hits the Earth in the form of sunshine over a stretch of only a few days. Talk about untapped potential.

Here in the U.S. our energy choices are the most important on the planet. We have only 5% of the world's population, yet we consume 25% of its energy. The coal and natural gas giants are pushing harder than ever in congress to keep carbon-emission standards lax and to block and complicate the construction of solar facilities in any way that they can. It is especially critical that we convert to renewable energies because this country still has massive oil reserves, and we are the "Saudi Arabia of coal" in the words of author Jeff Goodell, with a 250-year supply – the world's largest. Without a substantial and steady outcry against fossil fuels, these gargantuan polluters will continue to burn until these dirty fuels are essentially all gone.

By then, our planet will be unrecognizable and completely unlivable. All that may be left will be blackened skies, polluted waters and soils, a few suffering, stalwart animal and plant species, and a giant pile of cash. How long will we stand idly by while a few energy companies, in the words of author Elaine Smitha, "screw mother nature for profit? (20)" According to eminent biologist E.O. Wilson, 50% of plant and animal species on Earth will be extinct by 2100 (21). That may sound extreme, but I have criss-crossed five continents and studied and lectured about the physical geography of our planet for the past twenty years; please hear me when I say that we are rapidly plunging toward that reality.

Should we give more weight to professionals who care about and study the planet, or to an article in a popular magazine, a comment from a TV newscaster, or to an Exxon/Mobil commercial that makes it seem like their engineers are wise and prudent stewards of our earth? Likewise, should we trust our doctor when she tells us that our smoking and penchant for fried food will lead to a heart attack, or rather should we trust our friend who is "convinced" that there is no link between the two because he knows a few smokers who lived into old age?

On that note, nothing would make me happier than to know that the considerable capital, brilliant engineers, formidable CEOs, and genius PR firms of the fossil-fuel giants were actually focused on convincing and cajoling us to purchase solar or wind power in the same way that they promote oil or natural gas. It would be phenomenal if Shell, BP, Conoco-Phillips and Exxon/Mobil just woke up and internally decided of their own volition to earnestly move in an altruistic direction (rather than just give the idea beautifully marketed lip service). I have no doubt that many people within these companies have good intentions, and maybe even that voice inside that is pushing them to incite change. There is actually some evidence of this. Shell Oil is showing signs that they believe in renewable energy's future in that they periodically invest large sums in solar and wind production. Chevron and British Petroleum are following suit. Defense contractors such as Ceradyne, in lieu of supplying the military with industrial ceramics to be used as armor, has plans to manufacture solar-receiving apparatus when wartime ends (22).

I would love to make the oil-company Goliath into a friend and have all of his muscle working for our cause. Maybe someday soon – but more likely, the change will have to come from thousands and thousands of Davids who are aware and who demand the obvious and superior energy solution.

Oil companies seem determined to repeat the mistakes of the past. In 19th century Europe, despite supply limitations, plant strikes, and other problems with coal, European rulers and governments did not seek out alternative sources of energy but instead "hunkered down" and did their best to control and monopolize all that was left of this dwindling resource (23).

This is precisely what is happening with oil and coal in the 20th century. But now we have the option of solar power in our quiver, as well as the communication technology and democratic processes necessary to implement solar power on a grand scale. As conveyed earlier, I personally believe that converting to renewable energies, along with reducing meat consumption, are absolutely the two most powerful, positive changes that can be made on planet earth in coming years.

Trafficking in Sex

"Those who deny freedom to others deserve it not for themselves...This is a world of compensations; and he who would be no slave, must consent to have no slave."

-Abraham Lincoln, April 6, 1859, Letter to Henry Pierce

The following is a real-life profile taken from Campagna and Poffenberger's *The Sexual Trafficking in Children: an investigation of the child sex trade:*

"On August 1, 1984, an older white male was arrested by police officers of New York City's 7th Precinct for sexually abusing a nine-year-old Mexican boy. The child, Luis, had been registered two or three days earlier at a summer day camp on New York's lower east side by the same man.

An observant youth worker noticed that Luis was depressed, crying, and walking as though in pain. She took him aside and asked what was wrong. The story, as told to investigators from Defense for Children International – USA, was that Luis was born in Acapulco, Mexico. The father of his large and very poor family was approached three weeks before by a visiting Anglo who offered to take the boy to New York, provide him with an education, teach him English, and eventually find him a job. An unknown amount of money changed hands and Luis was brought to the United States, without proper documentation, past immigration officials. The effect on Luis of such a change in environment, from sunny Acapulco to the lower east side of New York, was doubtless traumatic. He had been separated from family, friends, school, and his entire way of life only to become a victim of sexual assault" (1).

Sex trafficking is the third largest source of income for organized crime – surpassed only by drugs and arms – generating between $25 and $32 billion each year (2)(3). It entails the voluntary and involuntary transportation of people across international borders in order to enter the sex trade. According to FBI and UNESCO general estimates, between 700,000 and two million people are trafficked each year worldwide (4)(5). Of those, approximately 70% are female and 50% are children (6). If non-trafficked women and children who enter the sex trade in their home country are included in this equation, the total numbers involved globally are much higher.

As I mentioned in the introduction, undergirding every trend is a set of widely held beliefs. In other words, behind every action there is an unseen source, be it a desire, a dream or a fear. Something as large as the international sex trade does not develop by accident; it is founded on a large set of thoughts, beliefs, and forces, which bring it into existence. Three salient attitudes and emotions that help to generate this pernicious industry are the judgment and repression of sexuality, desperation to survive amidst abject poverty in the developing world, and male chauvinism.

Repression of sex in many of the world's cultures limits and stifles sexuality, coaxing it to erupt in perversions and tweaked expressions such as sexual violence, pedophilia, the multi-billion dollar cyber-sex industry, and the sex trade. The U.S. is a somewhat ambivalent expression of this. Its Puritanical religious foundation inhibits many forms of sexual expression, yet the radio and television are flooded with explicit sexual messages and images. This both sensationalizes sex, yet at the same time cultivates a guilty conscience. In Europe, less of this polarization is seen.

Casual nudity is not uncommon on television, in films, and in popular magazines, but sex intertwined with power, drugs or violence is less prevalent. This subtle difference can be witnessed just by spending a few days in Paris, Madrid, or Rome. Does Europe's more moderate approach help to explain that the rate of sex crimes in Europe is two to three times lower than in the United States? (7). Perhaps.

Strict repression of sexuality, ironically, helps to generate the draw and profitability of the sex trade. Obviously, a completely liberal sexual environment is not ideal either. Yet regions where suppression, domination, and guilt related to sex are most prominent often display higher rates of sexually-transmitted disease (8).

The second attitude that perpetuates the sex trade is the utter desperation to survive in many third-world nations. Rising populations coupled with few options for income is the bleak reality in countless poor nations. Only desperation on this level could explain the tidal wave of both willing and unwilling participation in the sex trade. My many interviews of sex workers from Brazil to Kenya to Thailand bear this out. Some developed-world nations, such as parts of economically-depressed Eastern Europe, are also providing sex trade workers in large numbers.

The third belief or attitude is excessive masculine or "yang" energy, which leads to male chauvinism and domination. This yang (male, aggressive) energy dominating yin (female, passive) energy takes on several expressions. This energetic dynamic plays out even if both the patron/perpetrator and the object/victim are male, because the victim is still powerless, submissive, and dominated. Some even suggest that this interaction plays out between capitalism (yang) and the natural world (yin) (9)(10) as modern economies ravage nature to suit their appetites for raw materials and profit. Women and nature, in fact, are often coupled together both logistically and discursively since they both are posited to receive this masculine patriarchical domination (11)(12)(13).

In a traditional sense, this male domination of women also has very measurable social realities. The United Nations publishes a Gender Related Development Index (GDI) and a Gender Empowerment Measure (GEM), which are used in its annual Human Development Report to determine a country's level of gender equality. A score of 1.0 is perfect gender equality. Norway (0.94) topped the list, while Niger (0.26) was at the bottom. Many countries in Africa are in the 0.5 range, while most nations are between 0.6 and 0.75 globally (14). What this translates to is that women on this planet have less access to education, money, free expression, social status, and perhaps most of all, power.

Amidst the utter denigration of selling their bodies, women are also ironically elevated in importance because of their new role as providers for the family. In weak economies of the developing world, this increased income posits women on a new level in society. Despite the source of this money, sex workers often have pride in their observably moneyed status. They become the supporter of their families, including brothers and husbands. A notable Thai economist has estimated that the annual income generated by Thai sex workers in Japan alone is 310,500 million Yen, or U.S. $3.3 billion (15). Considering that in several destitute countries there are over a million female sex workers with a stream of income, this constitutes a gigantic shift in gender roles, and in the power of women in general.

While researching the sex industry in Thailand, I interviewed prostitutes, their "managers," and U.S. military personnel on leave in Thai port cities. When asked what their job was, several women were reticent to speak, but a few of these girls and women seemed to sit up straighter when they said, "I am a prostitute," almost with a glint of pride. When they learned that I was an American scholar researching the Thai economy and sex trade, two of the women even invited me to meet their parents and families.

One sex worker that I got to know on Phuket Island, a big tourist destination in southern Thailand, was nineteen-year-old Amina. Her presence and poise belied her youth; you'd swear you were talking to a thirty or thirty-five-year-old woman. One day I accepted an invitation to pray and meditate with Amina at a Buddhist temple on the island. It was a wonderful experience. Afterward she told me about her life goals, her dreams and about her very close relationship with her parents and brothers. I found Amina to be a strong, positive woman from a good family, and a person of good moral fabric. I was unable to look at the sex trade in the same way after getting to know her.

Amina voluntarily left her poor village in northeast Thailand to come to the city and make money in "any way that she could." She eventually ended up in Phuket, a big tourist destination several hours south of Bangkok. Many women do voluntarily enter the sex trade, but a huge proportion of them do so by coercion by a variety of methods including outright kidnapping and exportation, lure by phony job offers in foreign countries, or false marriage opportunities with Westerners advertised in local papers. Under these false pretenses, women accept transport to another country where the story changes. The transported women are told that they owe in upwards of 30,000 U.S. dollars for the cost of their transport, which they can pay off by working in sex bars or brothels. These women are essentially enslaved: monitored twenty-four hours a day and forced to acquiesce to all clients' demands. Debts are usually paid in a few to several months (16). Some organizations estimate that workers can earn their captors between $13,000 and $67,000 per year (17).

Debt dependence has been used as a tool of the dominant group, or "hegemon," throughout history and across cultures. After slavery ended in the United States, blacks in the south commonly entered into the sharecropping system in which they rented land at rates too high to be paid back with the crops that they grew, so they were perpetually in debt and subjected to the demands of the land owner. The IMF and World Bank sometimes use a very similar strategy with large loans to the developing world which allow the lending institutions to control and manipulate these economies at their will while debt dependence is in effect. Another parallel is that in the African slave trade and the modern sex trade, the wrangling and selling of local victims to Western powers is often facilitated by locals of the same tribe or ethnic group as the victim.

National governments play a role in the sex trade, as well – by turning a blind eye. Legal penalties for trafficking in humans are often minor compared to trafficking in arms or drugs. The lack of official acknowledgement of the sex trade itself precludes the granting of official "worker" visas to sex workers. This subjects them to all manner of human rights violations since sex workers are not protected by local law enforcement, nor eligible for public health care.

President Bush's approach, beginning in 2002, was a very aggressive policy designed to locate and punish traffickers in the U.S. (18). The approach of his predecessor, President Clinton, was much more focused on caring for victims' rights and developing better income opportunities for victims (19). A combination of these approaches would probably be ideal.

Globally, punishment of sex workers is still much more common than punishment of traffickers. In the case of Thai migrant workers in Japan, "if employers or traffickers are prosecuted at all, they are charged with immigration offenses, the employment of illegal aliens, or with operating an unlicensed entertainment business. They are almost never prosecuted for the severe human rights abuses they have committed, such as forced labor, illegal confinement, and physical violence" (20). Anti-prostitution or anti-illegal immigration laws directed at the victims only exacerbate the problem by increasing the profitability of the industry. On the contrary, in countries where prostitution is legal, trafficking is less common and the sex industry is more regulated (21).

The Asia Migrant Bulletin has documented the trafficking of migrants from the Philippines, Thailand, China, Indonesia, Burma, Sri Lanka, Bangladesh, India, Nepal, and of late from Vietnam, Laos, Cambodia, and Fiji. These sex workers were sent to the nations of Japan, Taiwan, Hong Kong, Macao, Malaysia, Singapore, Thailand, India, Australia, Europe, and the United States (22). "*Slumdog Millionaire*," which won the 2009 Oscar for best film of the year, highlights children who are forced into the sex trade in India. These may sound like exotic locales, but you may be as surprised as I was at how close to home this industry operates. I recently discovered that a major U.S. hub for sex trafficked girls and women is Oakland, California in the San Francisco bay area where I currently live and work. Many massage parlors in industrial/commercial sections of U.S. cities – usually ones with secured entry and opaque front windows – are the most common interface between trafficked individuals and their patrons.

Sex as an international business is tough to wipe out because if it is squelched in one area, it just reemerges elsewhere. This mobility is facilitated by organized crime syndicates around the globe, including gangs from Mexico, central America, and Russia as well as Chinese and Vietnamese triads, the Japanese Yakuza, South American drug cartels, and the Italian Mafia (23). For instance, Thailand and Sri Lanka have seen a diminishment of sex trade activity recently due to raised awareness and stronger laws, but this has been offset by an increase in activity in Latin America, the Caribbean, and Africa. These newly affected regions are "primed" for this invasion of money and domination because of their depressed economies and also due to the strong tradition of male dominance and patrilinealism in these areas.

Approximately 50,000 women from the Dominican Republic currently work abroad in the European sex industry (24). In the words of one sex trade researcher, "In the case of Dominican women, the proceeds from prostitution are used to support parents or children. For those women really concerned about providing such support, opportunities in the legal economy are very limited in a society where eighty dollars a month is the minimum salary for domestic work" (25).

With an undercurrent of so much repression and denouncement of sexuality imposed upon the women of the world, feelings of guilt, self-denial, sacrifice, and shame are not a surprising experience for women selling their bodies for sex. Also, from the other side of this equation, guilt, disregard, and domination are the energetic foundation of the (mostly, though not all, Western) men wanting to set loose their sexual desires on helpless or even coerced victims. None of the feelings and attitudes that these role players in the sex trade bring to an encounter could be described as positive, pleasant, or "healthy."

So let's follow that line of reasoning. It is widely accepted in the developed world that emotional and mental stress are the leading cause of illness. That is, one's mental and emotional state, more often than other factors, creates physical illness. Therefore it is certainly possible, and in fact plausible, that this massive stream of unhealthy emotions and mental attitudes that are infused into the sex trade may actually contribute to the physical manifestation of sexual diseases, including AIDS.

David R. Hawkins, M.D., Ph.D, is a world renowned psychiatrist and has also co-authored a book with Nobel Laureate Linus Pauling. On the metaphysics of AIDS, Dr. Hawkins writes, "Generally it appears that what's experienced as stress results in suppression of the thymus gland, and the body's defenses are consequently impaired. But the various research approaches to this topic fail to examine the relationship between belief systems and attitudes, and the resulting context of perception that determines the nature of individual experience" (26).

As stated earlier, regions where suppression, domination, and guilt related to sex are most prominent often display higher rates of disease. Legal and social openness about sex and the sex trade, for instance, results in psychological changes (empowerment and autonomy for women) and tangible changes (doctor visits and condom distribution), which can combine to lower transmission rates (27).

One extreme example is in southern Africa, which has the highest concentration of people with AIDS on Earth. In a few countries in this region, 20% or more of the adult population has the disease (28). I saw this first-hand when, on a bus passing through Uganda in the late 90s, I glimpsed a giant admonishing sign posted on the roadside as we approached a town which read simply "One-third of this town has HIV." Of note, women's rates of AIDS in the region often approach double that of men's. If we look at the extreme "dis-ease" with sex that women in the region have imposed upon them, the prominence of sex-related disease is perhaps more understandable.

In the words of Pulitzer-Prize winning science author Laurie Garrett, who has been covering the AIDS epidemic since the mid-1990s, "The number-one driving force for this epidemic in Sub Saharan Africa and increasingly in Asia is the extraordinarily low power balance on the side of females. Most women have no right of refusal of sexual intercourse. They have no ability to dictate when, where or with whom they have sex. Rape is so commonplace that it is only recently being thought of as a criminal activity" (29).

This energy of sexual suppression and mistreatment among women is so extreme and visceral in Africa that it frequently results in the death of women. A woman who commits adultery is often severely beaten or burned and fiercely judged or ostracized. In situations of infidelity, the murder of a woman by her husband is often not strictly forbidden or monitored. Rape is so common that many marriages begin when a woman is raped by an acquaintance. Rape is also a tool of demoralization and power, which is commonly utilized in civil wars on the continent. One cultural phenomenon in sub-Saharan Africa – female genital mutilation, or female circumcision – is a vivid and extreme example of sexual mistreatment. Often at the age of eight to ten, young girls in Africa have their clitoris scraped off with blunt, traditional, non-medical instruments. The procedure is called "purification" because of its effect of diminishing the woman's ability to experience sexual pleasure, thereby lowering her libido and better ensuring fidelity to her husband.

UNICEF estimates that 70 million girls aged 15-49 in Africa and the Middle East have undergone the procedure (30). Although sixteen African nations now ban the practice (31), approximately three million new girls still face the prospect of female circumcision each year (32). This level of sexual suppression and physical abuse aligns with the general precepts of the sex trade, making African women very susceptible to the industry.

A true story of a victim of the sex industry may elucidate the larger problem even better. Throughout my travels and research, I have encountered many girls and women who find themselves at the mercy of circumstance: destitute, with a lack of education and opportunity, and confronted with the sole promising yet uninspiring option of selling one's own body. A conversation that I had with two girls in Nairobi, Kenya in the late 90s had a profound affect on me.

"They can't be older than fifteen," I remember saying to myself when I saw two school girls strolling a boulevard in the outskirts of the two-million-plus metropolis in southern Kenya. Their aggressive, over-confident stares propositioning male passers-by divulged their profession. Having just finished my first year of teaching at an inner-city high school in Los Angeles, I thought these two girls looked like sophomores in my class that should be talking about homework or the prom. My heart went out to them, and I had to reach out. I walked up to them and, just to be sure, asked if they were prostitutes. Without a hint of shame, they both nodded.

111

"I have a question to ask but I'm not sure how to ask it," I said. Their eyebrows raised, waiting. I continued. "Wouldn't you rather just work at the post office or at a bank or a restaurant, rather than have to risk so much out here?"

The more courageous of the two immediately took a step toward me and pointed her index finger at me. "I will tell you why we don't have jobs like that." Her boldness took me aback. As she continued, her East African accent was more detectable. "My motha is a teacha and she makes feefty dollars a month. I have already made feefty dollars *tooday*, and on a good day I will make 200 dollars." I found myself with nothing to say. It's tough to argue with a disparity like that, so I just nodded and said "Well… be safe out here," and I left.

My heart sank more with every step as I fully comprehended the inevitability of their situation. It is the prerogative of citizens in nations that have the power to make change not only to police traffickers who force women and children into the sex trade, but also to earnestly work to change the social and economic circumstances that allow this industry to thrive.

Addicted to Dirty Fuels, By Design

"Peace is for the women and the weak; empires are forged by war."

**- King Agamemnon as played by Brian Cox
in the 2004 motion picture "Troy"**

What's ONE thing you can do?
Going solar or driving a high-mileage, hybrid or electric car are the most powerful ways to lessen this country's addiction to fossil fuels. You can also vote against any legislation that would further the oil, natural gas, or coal industries.

In the summer of 2008 I was flying from Houston to Los Angeles next to an oil industry engineer and salesman whom I found quite glib. We spoke at length about oil, coal, and natural gas, but it was difficult to get more than a few words out of him when the topic of renewable energy came up.

"I know oil reservoirs are drying up pretty quickly," I said to him, gauging his response. "When your best sites start to run out of oil, you could probably make a lot of money tapping solar or wind power on those exact same sites."

"Maybe," he said, "but we're not tooled for that. We're tooled for oil. When sites dry up, we just search farther and dig deeper."

His unwavering focus – well, fixation – on oil actually surprised me. But then I realized that this describes much of the world. You, reading this book, and I, writing this book, are both dependent on oil. Our lives cannot function without it. This did not happen by accident; rather, our dependence has been cultivated by meticulous and often insidious design. The political subterfuge and environmental harm that the petroleum industry has espoused affects nearly every aspect of our lives every single day, down to the air we breathe and the food that we eat.

But before we get into the negatives of the oil industry, let's look at the substantial *positives* – because they are still meaningful. Oil tycoons, engineers and developers over the last 150 years have played a huge role in the industrial revolution and in the development of transportation via automobile and airplane. Until the 1850s, America's urban areas were lit by street lights that burned whale blubber oil until kerosene, refined from petroleum, was first used. In the beginning of the 20th century, the U.S. already led the world in oil production, and gasoline fueled Ford's automobiles as well as the planes and ships that defeated Hitler's Germany. As early as the 1930s, American companies such as Texaco and Rockefeller's Standard Oil spread cutting edge drilling technology around the world, extracting oil in locations like Saudi Arabia and offshore in the Persian Gulf.

The ingenuity, ambition, and technical skill of oil producers over the last century and a half has allowed for giant surges in economic output and the fixation of critical global technological advancements. Though companies from Holland, Russia, the UK, Venezuela, and Brazil, for instance, are major oil producers, U.S. companies have always and continue to dominate the industry. John D. Rockefeller, in particular, saw an emerging market niche in the mid-19th century and he capitalized on it. That ingenuity and market responsiveness is intrinsic to American greatness. What if American companies had dragged their feet and remained entrenched in the whale blubber industry, allowing other nations to gain an insurmountable lead in petroleum production? That would have affected our economic prowess for the entire 20th century.

Well, the same scenario is playing out today with renewable energies, but this time we are slow to respond. Renewable energies are the fastest growing energy source on the planet by far, yet the U.S. remains overly committed to anachronistic fossil fuels. Oil moved the world forward and vaulted the U.S. upward economically, but a new era in energy is emerging now. Besides the fact that there is astronomically more money to be made in renewables, pollution from fossil fuels is choking the planet. It's critical that consumers, such as you and I, fully absorb how consistently and thoroughly oil pollutes our beautiful planet.

As a planet we burn about one trillion gallons of oil annually, which releases nineteen trillion pounds of carbon dioxide into our skies (1)(2). Countless cities worldwide now have unsafe levels of smog, causing a huge rise in asthma and emphysema rates, especially in industrialized countries. The World Health Organization estimates that some 350,000 people die every year in East Asia alone as a result of urban airborne pollution, which is largely comprised of carbon emissions. Also, even though these events are rarely publicized, oil tankers and deep water oil wells are constantly spilling and leaking oil. About thirty million gallons of oil have spilled into our oceans **every year** since 1970 (3). In some years, ten times that amount has been spilled.

To put that in perspective, I called my friend Jerald who helps to prevent and clean up spills for Exxon Mobile. He said that if you spill a cup of oil into the ocean, it can spread out to cover the equivalent of an acre of water. Just imagine if you spilled 1,000 gallons of oil. How about thirty million gallons? In the ocean, tens of thousands of square miles are regularly coated with oil and every fish or bird that goes into or out of the water is coated with that oil and will likely die due to inability to breath, fly, or clean itself. Thirty million gallons is the average amount spilled every year on the planet, and general estimates suggest that it takes fifty years to fully clean up a spill of that size. How is it possible that hardly a shred of this onslaught of petroleum spills is ever reported to the public? Sounds a bit insidious to me. But that's only the beginning.

As I am writing this, the sole of my right foot is stained by some oil sludge that I stepped on while running on the beach here in Los Angeles a few days ago. Oil spills don't just disappear, and evidence of them washes ashore all over the world every day.

Since we all play a part in this addiction to oil, it is our prerogative to at least *know* what we are doing, to say nothing of actually changing our lifestyle or challenging the powers-that-be. Please indulge me as we look beyond the environmental degradation caused by oil to the war, censorship, subterfuge, and deceit, which has moved this substance into prevalence.

Beginning in World War II, when oil embargoes against Axis powers were critical to their defeat, the United States realized how critical a steady supply of oil was to its livelihood. The first administration of George W. Bush made oil acquisition a top priority, for example, and identified two main potential sources of petroleum. First, in efforts to transport oil from the Caspian Sea to friendly ports in Pakistan, an oil pipeline had to pass through Afghanistan. Yet the Taliban was against the pipeline. Second, Iraq's third largest oil reserves on Earth were attractive, but despotically guarded by Saddam Hussein. All that was needed was an "entrance strategy" into these countries. Then, only a few months after Bush took office, the twin towers and the Pentagon were attacked. Suddenly we had a reason to rally public support for an invasion. The final report of the 9/11 Commission cited that specific members of the Bush administration deliberately used 9/11 as justification to invade Iraq (4). Even the Oliver Stone-directed movie "W" was transparent about the Bush team's plan to acquire Iraq's oil by any means necessary.

Because of the gravity of the event and the fact that it was proven to be related to oil acquisition, 9/11 deserves much more investigation and contemplation, which it will not likely receive. A few independent documentaries about 9/11 are very eye-opening for anyone interested in deeper layers to the events. The film *Fahrenheit 9/11* has copious galvanizing information, and *Loose Change,* another documentary, is a very powerful exposé into the scientific explanation of the Twin Tower collapses. More importantly, these documentaries represent information on 9/11 *from a non-mainstream source.* A critical detail that these films delve into is that no high-rise building in history with a steel frame has ever completely collapsed due to fire, nor from being struck by an airplane. Also, a third building called Seven World Trade Center, which was a block away and was not struck by an airplane, unexplainably also caught fire and collapsed on the same day.

To say that 9/11 was a surprise to everyone in our government is very difficult to support. Even U.S. intelligence agencies predicted the attack, but no significant precautions were taken. A few months before September 11, 2001, a briefing to Dick Cheney and George Bush read:

Based on a review of all sources reporting over the last five months, we believe that UBL will launch a significant terrorist attack against the U.S. and/or Israel's interests in the coming weeks. The attack will be spectacular and designed to inflict mass casualties against U.S. facilities or interests. Attack preparations have been made. Attack will occur with little or no warning (5).

Two months later 9/11 occurred, and several events immediately ensued which had little to do with terrorism and everything to do with oil acquisition in the Caspian region. Within three months of 9/11, U.S. ambassadors met with the Pakistani oil minister, Taliban-occupied Kabul was taken by U.S. military, Hamid Karzai was sworn in as the new Afghan president, and construction of the oil pipeline through Afghanistan officially began. Such a moment of national crisis seems like a strange time to urgently need to meet with the Pakistani oil minister and begin building an oil pipeline. But in all the hubbub, scarcely anyone noticed.

Then we shifted our gaze to Iraq. Spearheaded by U.S. interests, in 2002, the UN Security Council began the search for "weapons of mass destruction" in Iraq (6). Soon, several comments by White House officials began to link 9/11 to Iraq, including a statement by Dick Cheney on National Public Radio in January, 2003: "There's overwhelming evidence (that) there was a connection between Al Qaeda and the Iraq government" (7). No such evidence was ever provided.

It should be said that a government going to lengths to care for the needs of its citizens is a worthy endeavor. The two presidential administrations of George W. Bush showed themselves to be efficacious, powerful, and single-minded about their acquisition of oil to supply our domestic demand. Energy has to come from somewhere, and they "got the job done," as it were, by any means necessary. That kind of effectiveness is critical to the functioning of a government. Neither worthy nor necessary, however, were the very questionable invasions of Afghanistan and Iraq, and the trillions of tax dollars spent in order to pay for these oil wars.

Waging war is, unfortunately, far from the end of the desperate measures to which some will go in order to acquire more oil. "There's not a lot of easy oil left to be found," says Matt Elmer, operations manager for Conoco Phillips, "otherwise we would have found it… Right now we are pushing out to more remote areas, pushing out to deeper waters, whether it's the Gulf of Mexico or offshore Alaska" (8). The "oil sands" of Alberta, Canada is a region where companies are literally bulldozing trees in order to excavate oil-saturated soil and squeeze every last drop from it. The Dalai Lama himself, along with Desmond Tutu and seven other Nobel Peace Laureates, wrote a personal letter to President Obama asking him to block the Keystone oil pipeline, which connects these oil sands to refineries and ports in Texas. The disaster waiting to happen is that the pipeline passes through the Ogallala aquifer, which holds a large proportion of America's fresh groundwater supply.

In the great central valley of California, Chevron has already extracted most of the "sweet" crude oil and now all that is left is denser, thicker petroleum, which is too viscous to be pumped to the surface. Rather than just looking upwards and capturing the abundant sunshine and wind in California with panels and turbines, the oil giant is plunging super-heated steam into these deep wells in order to soften the oil enough to remove it. According to the National Geographic Channel, this requires 81 trillion BTUs of energy every day, which is enough to power an air conditioner for every person on Earth (9). Clearly this process is requiring more energy than it is producing, which manifests the inherent desperation and lack of economic and environmental logic.

"Deepwater Horizon" is a name that is now emblazoned in the minds of every American. In April of 2010, some fifty miles off the coast of New Orleans, British Petroleum's mile-deep well ruptured and began to spew millions of gallons of oil per day. It took BP three months to cap the geyser, but not before 180 million gallons of oil were released, making it one of the largest – and most publicized – spills in global history. The leak has severely degraded the regional ecosystem and depressed the fishing economy of the Gulf States. As a comparison, there are no catastrophic spills of wind or sunshine, nor are there any significant negative effects on the environment from renewables such as solar, wind, wave, or geothermal energy.

If the BP explosion and spill got your attention, you should know that there were 858 *other* oil well explosions and fires in the past ten years, and there are currently almost 4,000 oil wells in the Gulf of Mexico alone (10). That's a huge number of accidents and a giant potential for many, many more.

And have you heard of the globally infamous Exxon Valdez oil tanker crash of 1989 in which ten million gallons of oil were spilled along the pristine coast of Alaska? It may be surprising to know that thirty-three even larger oil spills occurred *before* the Exxon Valdez, and there have been fifteen larger spills in the years since (11). Yet this topic is conspicuously and consistently absent from news programming.

If I were to list all of the pipeline leaks, ocean tanker spills, and oil well "accidents" that have occurred, they would fill an entire book. It is relentless, overwhelming, and unconscionable the amount of oil that pollutes our water and land *before* it even gets to the consumer to be burned and turned into air pollution! Well-paid conservative political lobbyists are constantly trying to dismiss, avoid, and downplay this simple fact in order to protect profits for the fossil fuel giants. Oil and coal companies *do* boost economic numbers and employ thousands upon thousands of people in the U.S. alone, but they also pollute and spoil our waterways, our land, and our air, which is the foundation of our food supply, our economy, and our livelihood. Other sources of energy don't force us to make this Faustian bargain.

"But if we stop using oil, it will hurt our economy," a student of mine interjected during class one day. I instantly thought of a sex trafficker whom I spoke to, with guaranteed anonymity, who said, "If the police stop our business in this part of Thailand, everyone will suffer because we *are* the economy. What will people do for money then?" It is clear that some industries are so deplorable that they need to be mitigated on moral, environmental, and social grounds, even if they are indeed profitable. Besides, solar power already employs more people than the oil extraction industry, as stated in a previous chapter, so more sustainable jobs are waiting for those who leave dirty fossil fuel production.

It is absolutely essential to oil companies that the public is not made aware of this wicked dichotomy. Due to covert pressure from oil powers, U.S. media often plays the role of accomplice to oil-industry public relations groups in suppressing the connection between fossil-fuel burning and global warming (12). "We did make the link to global warming once," said one TV news editor, "but it triggered a barrage of complaints from the Global Climate Coalition to our top network executives" (The GCC was the oil and coal lobbying group) (13). The absence of this link to global warming leaves a critical gap, which is elucidated by authors Maxwell and Jules Bykoff:

"Since the general public garners most of its knowledge about science from the mass media . . . the disjuncture between scientific discourse and popular discourse (is responsible for the fact that) significant and concerted international action has not been taken to curb practices that contribute to global warming" (14).

This suppression goes past the media and into the realm of government. According to the EPA, in 2003, four paragraphs were removed from its report on the environmental effects of climate change on the US after the White House had access to it (15). Also, by 2003, ExxonMobil was giving more than one million dollars a year to an array of ideological, right-wing organizations opposing action on climate change, including the Competitive Enterprise Institute, and Frontiers of Freedom (16).

Most of us are aware of many of the negative effects of oil, but the problems associated with coal are even less publicized. Yet each one of us burns coal every day of our lives. In fact, if you're sitting in a room with the lights on, you are most likely burning coal right now. A few shocking statistics help to tell the egregious story of coal.

Since 1900, over 100,000 individuals have died in coal-mining accidents globally and another 200,000 were taken by black lung from years of inhaling the toxic air in coal mines (17). That's more deaths than America suffered in the entirety of

World War I. Twenty thousand coal miners die every year in China alone, including about ten per week that die in the construction of new mines (18). Also, in the eastern United States, hundreds of mountain tops in the Appalachians have been sliced off at the top in order to access the coal inside them and over 1,200 miles of streams have been completely buried with the resultant debris (19). And those are just the drawbacks of *mining* the coal. Burning it has released so much toxicity into the air that it is estimated to have shortened the lives of a half million Americans.

Oil and coal are thought of as the "dirtier" fossil fuels, but natural gas isn't exactly squeaky clean either. Bonnie and Truman Burnett had plans to retire in their dream cottage in rural Pennsylvania until the wastewater from a natural gas well on an adjacent property killed all of the fish in their pond and ruined a large section of forest (20). Most natural gas is obtained through the process of "fracking," whereby a toxic mix of chemicals is pumped into porous rock deep underground, which fractures the rock and releases the gas. The chemicals absorb the gas and the mix is pumped back to the surface. This generates billions of gallons of toxic waste liquid from the thousands of such wells in Pennsylvania alone, resulting in over 1,000 reports of water contamination near drill sites already (21). Shockingly, a provision in the 2005 U.S. energy bill, called the "Halliburton loophole" because the gas giant's former CEO Dick Cheney was Vice President when it passed, forbids the E.P.A. from regulating the fracking process in any way. I think that qualifies as insidious, don't you?

This makes me remember the words of a good friend of mine named Tony whose roofing company I worked for as a salesman during summertime in college. Tony would tell customers to consider the true *cost* of a cheap roof, rather than just the price. "Your roof is protecting everything precious that you own, including your family. You can't afford a cheap roof because the actual cost is too high." Authors Martin Katzman and Travis Bradford agree with Tony when it comes to our sources of energy. They describe the pollution, death, and war caused by using fossil fuels as "social costs" which must be included when energy prices are discussed (22). We have become so used to these negative effects that we forget that they are tied to fossil fuels, not an intrinsic part of human life. They virtually disappear when we choose renewable energy to power our world.

In his February 1, 2012 appearance on *The Daily Show*, Brad Pitt said "If we invented the automobile today...would we say 'I know, we'll run it on a finite fossil fuel, we'll export a half a trillion dollars of our GDP, we'll spend hundreds of billions of dollars on our military to protect that interest, *and* it'll deplete the environment?'"

On a personal note, my great uncle, a hard-working Austrian immigrant named Michael Fleishacker, had his career brought to an end by big oil. Michael worked as an engineer for L.A.'s largest electric light rail system until a conglomerate of General Motors, Standard Oil, and Firestone Tires bought it out in the 1950s. The "Pacific Electric," as it was called, was an incredibly extensive network of railways stretching sixty miles inland and along approximately seventy miles of urban development on the coast. The company was totally bought out and dismantled by 1961, and the largest urban car center on the planet was born. There are now twelve million cars in Southern California, which up until the 1990s was more than the total in any foreign country. A very similar buyout and dismantling of public transportation systems occurred in approximately sixty other U.S. cities.

In summation, the power of the dirty fuels oligarchy, which combines oil, coal, natural gas, and nuclear power, is based on the fact that these are all controllable finite resources, and therefore they provide excellent opportunities for monopolization and profit. And oil companies alone receive about $4 billion a year in federal subsidies. Together with members of government, the dirty fuels oligarchy manipulates public perception, invades foreign nations for resources, and obscures the link between fossil fuel burning and global warming.

Their powerful lobbies fight tooth and nail against legally lowering carbon emissions and tightening environmental standards simply because it would temporarily reduce profits. All the while abundant, clean, renewable energy technologies have been actively suppressed for decades. The result, very simply, is that the United States and much of the globe is dependent on fossil fuels, by design.

The Rise of Women

"When you save the women, you save the world."

- Mary J. Blige, R&B recording artist (2)

"...there is no tool for development more effective than the education of girls. No other policy is as likely to raise economic productivity, lower infant and maternal mortality, improve nutrition and promote health, including the prevention of HIV/AIDS."

- Former UN Secretary General, Kofi Anan

The Third Way to Save the Planet: Uplift Women
Women are heavily repressed in much of the developing world, which denies them basic rights and cripples their societies' development. Women's ability to be educated, vote, and own property has myriad positive effects on a society including reduction in birth rates, child mortality, and domestic abuse, as well as an increase in literacy (1). The feminine perspective and presence at all levels of society is critical for the planet to move forward in its evolution. This inevitable rebalancing of our very human nature – within every person and every nation – entails less focus on aggression and domination and more espousal of compassion, communication, and interdependence. We must hold our women on high and encourage our daughters to be leaders of the next generation. Salient organizations that support women are UNICEF, Women For Women International, and CARE. Engaging and supporting the essence and power of women will highlight and cultivate the grandest version of humanity's future.

On May 7, 1919, Maria Eva Duarte was born to a single mother in a small, impoverished town in rural Argentina. One of five young children, Eva had to work as a cook and a maid in order to help support the family. Despite her mother's intentions of marrying off her pretty daughter to a well-established bachelor, at the age of fifteen and without formal education, Eva left for the big city of Buenos Aires to pursue her dream of acting.

After her professional debut in the play *The Perezes Misses*, Eva's career took off. She acted in movies, toured with theatre companies, and became one of the highest paid radio personalities in the country. At the age of 25, then Eva Duarte attended a fundraising event where she met Juan Perón, the Minister of Labor. They soon married and within a few years Perón was elected President of Argentina.

Eva Perón, affectionately known by Argentines as "Evita," immediately began sitting in on Peron's high level strategy meetings, at the suggestion of the president himself. Her political acumen coalesced quickly and within a year, in 1947, she had pushed through a bill that gave women the right to vote for the first time in Argentina. Evita also spearheaded many altruistic organizations and even founded the country's first women's political party which rose to a half million members. During her time as First Lady and while still in her twenties, she also traveled throughout Europe, having a private audience with the Pope and several heads of state.

Mrs. Perón rose to the level of national hero but then sadly succumbed to cancer at the age of thirty-three. Perhaps due to her influence, when her husband was re-elected president two decades later, he chose his new wife as his Vice-Presidential running mate. After Juan Perón died in office in 1974, his wife, Isabel Martinez de Perón, then became the first female head of state in the Western hemisphere.

Eva Perón is an example of how the rise of one woman can lift up an entire nation and change the course of history. The world is at a turning point where more emphasis on a female approach and sensibility are essential in order for us to move to a higher level of social functioning. More specifically, an expansion of the communicative female "yin" energy is needed to balance out an excess of aggressive male "yang" energy on the planet. A big hindrance to this is the fact that in most of the world, females are still second-class citizens in several very real, measurable ways.

Women own a paltry one percent of the land on the planet (3). Eighty million fewer females than males are currently enrolled in school across the globe, and even in the most progressive industrialized countries, women are far from income parity in the job market (4). In every nation but one, women could not vote until the 20th century (5), and in several Middle Eastern countries, women still have only partial voting rights or none at all. Most shocking is that one in three women on the planet are raped or physically beaten within their lifetime (6). In fact, more women die from domestic violence than from war, traffic accidents, malaria, and cancer combined (7).

The economic marginalization of women, it could be said, is as harmful as any other form of repression. According to the UN, women earn only 10% of the world's income (8). This is true despite the fact that in most cultures women perform the majority of household and childrearing duties, and in the developing world, women are responsible for up to 80% of local food production (9). I noticed in my travels and it is well documented that in the poorest nations, women and children spend inordinate amounts of time just collecting water and firewood every day. This often precludes children's attendance in school and prohibits mothers from seeking employment outside the home.

One success story is told well by New York Times Op-Ed columnist Nicolas Kristof (10). He writes of Jane Ngoiri, a 38-year-old single mom who dropped out of school after the eighth grade, then was later abandoned by her husband when she had two small children to support. About ten years ago, while still supporting herself by selling her body on the streets, she joined an organization called "Jamii Bora," which in Swahili means "Good Families." It focuses on microfinance loans and entrepreneurship training.

In Kristof's words, "Jane learned to sew, left prostitution and used her savings and a small loan to buy a sewing machine. She began buying secondhand wedding gowns and bridesmaid dresses for about $7 each, and then cutting them up to make two or three smaller dresses. Jane's business flourished, and she used her profits to buy a small home in a safe suburb and to keep her children in school." Her eldest daughter, Caroline, has graduated from high school, and her son Anthony is ranked 1st out of 138 students at a prestigious boarding school in Kenya. Thankfully, exceptions like Jane are becoming increasingly common.

But women's struggles for advancement are not limited to the developing world. In wealthy countries, dual-income households with children also often see mothers working full-time and silently taking responsibility for a larger share of raising the children in an unspoken contract that gender-divides labor. And in the labor market, women still earn markedly less than men. As of 2015, census data shows that full-time employed women earn 77% as much as full-time employed men in the United States. The gender gap is much wider in the Asian nations of Japan, Republic of

Korea, Malaysia, and Singapore, where women earn approximately half that of men (11). Notably, race still has a significant effect on the income of women in the United States. In 2013, Latina women in the U.S. earned an average of $541/week, African-American women earned $606/week, white women earned $722/week, and Asian-Amercan women made $819/week (12).

Researcher Janet Momsen believes that one disadvantage for women is that they are often concentrated in the informal sector, in jobs such as maids and street vendors, which is very insecure. Also, heavily female-dominated jobs (such as nurse, secretary, and school teacher) become categorically devalued and hence of less earning power (13).

As a teacher, I know that education is the most important tool for ensuring the rise of women, especially the poor. Across the planet, tens of millions of fewer girls are enrolled in school than boys (14), resulting in the fact that 64% of all illiterate adults are women (15). These statistics are due to a host of factors including disenfranchisement, lack of basic rights, male-dominated societies, and simply the burden of child rearing and household management – all of which lessen women's access to education.

In Africa, the Middle East, and South Asia more boys attend primary school than girls (16). At the high-school level in the developing world, the gender gap widens, with over half of girls not attending school in west and central Africa and 15% not attending in Latin America (17). The number of men in college in the developing world nearly doubles that of women (18). But it's interesting that in industrialized countries, the story is quite different; approximately equal numbers of males and females attend school at all levels, except in universities where females are more present (19).

Kenyan Wangari Maathai's story is an excellent illustration of the power of education. In 1959, Senator John F. Kennedy agreed to support a program known as "Airlift Africa" which brought hundreds of top Kenyan scholars to universities in the United States. One of those students was a young woman named Wangari Maathai who went on to earn her bachelor's degree from Mt. Scholastica College in Kansas and her Master's from the University of Pittsburgh. But she did not stop there. Eventually Wangari completed her doctoral studies in veterinary biology and thus became the first East African woman ever to receive a Ph.D. In the late 1970s, Professor Maathai founded the Green Belt Movement which focused on women's rights, anti-poverty efforts, and environmentalism. One tangible product of the movement was the successful planting of forty million trees in the East African region.

Despite consistent battles against sexism and prejudice in her home nation of Kenya, her altruistic efforts earned Wangari Maathai the 2004 Nobel Peace Prize. The forward thinking of Senator John F. Kennedy gave a head start to this amazing woman, who went on to set precedents and crash through barriers that would improve the East African environment and social structure forever.

In doing this research, I was amazed at how clearly the statistics showed that educating women improved both their communities and the world. In the words of former UN Secretary General, Kofi Anan:

"Study after study has taught us that there is no tool for development more effective than the education of girls. No other policy is as likely to raise economic productivity, lower infant and maternal mortality, improve nutrition and promote health, including the prevention of HIV/AIDS."

The average literate woman marries later, is more likely to get a paid job, and has larger social webs, all of which give her more decision-making power in her own home (20)(21)(22). Educated women also understand hygiene and family planning better, so more of their children survive, causing them to need to have fewer children overall (23). In fact, across the developing world, every 10% that the female literacy rate increases, the total fertility rate decreases by about one-half child per woman (24). This is significant because the population is escalating particularly rapidly in developing countries. Moreover, when you educate a woman, you educate an entire family, because women are statistically much more likely than men to teach other family members to read.

A debate over the relative strengths and weaknesses of men as compared to women has existed for millennia. And despite sharing over 99% of their genetic code, men and women do have quantifiable physical differences. Men, for instance, are usually physically larger and stronger, while women mature measurably faster than men, based on hormonal and brain activity. More specifically, the prefrontal cortex, which guides and controls emotions, is larger and matures more rapidly in women, while the anterior cingulated cortex, which weighs options and assesses decisions, is also larger in females (25). Physical strength and aggression translated to security and prosperity for millennia. But today, when reason, wise decision-making, and productive management of one's emotions are critical capacities for CEOs, diplomats, and leaders, women are shining more brightly, and more often stepping into the lead role. Today over twenty prominent nations have female heads of state, including Germany, Argentina, Chile, South Korea, Switzerland, and Senegal.

I believe that female leadership is absolutely essential for our future. This made me look into the topic a bit further. It turns out that hundreds of studies have been conducted about the relative leadership styles of men and women from around the globe. A broad conclusion is that men were found to lead with a "transactional" style which focuses on delegating tasks to subordinates and rewarding compliance with money in a contractual exchange. Aggression, domination, and the use of force elicit success in such a system (26). Women were found to lead in a "transformational" style that highlights interpersonal relationships, inspiration, and uplifting feedback (27). Most importantly, while women and men did not appear to differ in their effectiveness as leaders, women were "less concerned with personal power and more concerned with the organization as a whole" (28).

Most women of the world, however, are forgotten at the other end of the social hierarchy. Business leaders often proclaim that caring for the environment, women, and the neediest among us is contrary to producing economic growth. Yet authors Gita Sen, Adrienne Germain and Lincoln Chen warn against this.

"Approaches to economic growth and ecological sustainability must be such as to secure livelihoods, basic needs, political participation, and women's reproductive rights, not to work against them. Thus, environmental policies and programs must support and sustain livelihoods and basic needs, not counterpose "nature" against the survival needs of the most vulnerable people in the present" (29).

I deeply believe it to be a fallacy that protecting nature and the disenfranchised, especially women, is a hindrance to the economy. When protected and healthy, the one billion poorest people on the planet, along with the environment, are vastly more productive, strong, and buoyant. This is simultaneously good for economic output and sustainable growth. And in terms of our true *resources*, the wisdom and participation of women is perhaps the largest untapped resource of this era. In the words of Mahatma Gandhi,

"If only the women of the world came together, they could display such heroic nonviolence as to kick away the atom bomb like a mere ball. If the women of Asia wake up they will dazzle the world. My experiment in nonviolence would be instantly successful if I could secure women's help" (30).

Taking a more capital-driven approach to helping the plight of women, by late 1993, thirty-five of forty-six African countries had received loans from the IMF and World Bank aimed at economic development. But certain programs which were mandatory aspects of the loans have been found to actually undercut the progress of women (31). These "structural adjustment programs," or SAP, essentially shift a nation's economy from being domestically focused (trade of goods and services within a country) to being internationally focused (exported goods).

The work of women is therefore instantly devalued because they do the lion's share of domestic, unskilled, and untradeable labor. These adjustment policies also pull huge monies out of public services such as education, infrastructure development, and health care, and put it toward resource extraction and export-focused production. This directly and negatively affects those dependent on public services, especially women. Relatedly, many health-care systems have become largely privatized, as in the case in Nigeria, which is now fee-for-service (32). This has a huge negative impact on the availability and quality of reproductive and child-rearing care for women.

In 2010, I attended Amnesty International's annual conference in San Francisco, hoping to connect and collaborate with other like-minded people. During the three-day event I sat in on one particular presentation by supermodel-turned-activist Christy Turlington-Burns that opened my eyes to the critical importance of reproductive health in the lives of women throughout the world. Christy spoke and showed us clips of her movie *No Woman, No Cry* in which she travels around the world capturing harrowing stories about the disparity between the birthing experience in rich and poor nations.

Approximately half a million women die annually in the developing world from childbirth-related issues. That is one death every minute. Two-thirds of those deaths occur in Subsaharan Africa, and most of the remainder occur in India (33). Filming an East African woman in the midst of severe pregnancy complications, Christy and her production crew broke down and paid the paltry $20 needed for a van ride to a distant hospital which saved the lives of both the woman and her child. Over a lifetime, a woman's chance of dying during childbirth in Subsaharan Africa is 1 in 22, as opposed to 1 in 8,000 in industrialized countries (34). This means that in most of Africa, a woman having a baby has only slightly better chances of surviving than if she played Russian roulette with a loaded gun.

A woman's access to reproductive health care is essential to building healthy communities and nations, but this access is often limited by strongly paternalistic societies (35)(36). You may have read the story a few years ago about the ten-year-old bride, Nujood Ali, who walked into a courthouse in her native Yemen and stated "I came to get a divorce." Her parents had married her off to a man in his thirties who beat her and demanded sex daily. Despite her pleading, the child bride's parents refused to come to her aid, but a female lawyer eventually did take the case. Nujood was eventually granted a divorce, and she is now fifteen years old, living with an aunt and attending school.

Even though Nujood's story ended well, it's important to remember that a full sixty million women alive today have had an arranged marriage, meaning that they tend to marry and have children at a much younger age (37). One simple fact makes this pertinent – women under the age of fifteen who have children are *five* times more likely to die in childbirth than women in their twenties (38). So allowing women to mature and "come of age" a bit more before marriage and childbirth has many statistical benefits.

Religion, unfortunately, can also be a hindrance to women's control over their own health and reproduction. Extreme sects of any religion often tend toward strict paternalism. Author Aziza Ahmed writes about the irony of Islamic countries' fierce opposition to U.S. military aggression, yet an alignment with that aggression if it is directed against women (39).

Pope Benedict XVI has said that Africa's AIDS problem will not be solved by condoms, but in fact, exacerbated by them (40). Yet only 23% of couples in Subsaharan Africa use contraception, as compared to 61% in the developing world in general (41). It is no surprise then that two-thirds of all HIV cases, and three-fourths of all women on Earth who are HIV positive are found in Subsaharan Africa (42).

The list of challenges facing women in their global plight goes on and on, but I am so passionate about this issue that I must also mention what is probably the most heinous act committed against women: sexual abuse and rape. This prevalent crime is also one of the most under-reported. In a recent international study, the percentage of women who had been sexually abused by their *regular partner* was 59% in Ethiopia, 30% in Thailand, 14% in Brazil, and 6% in Japan (43). A bit surprisingly, with non-intimate partners, the rates were much lower.

The act of rape is also very commonly used during wartime as a tool for demoralization, abuse of power, and genetic decimation of a rival ethnic group. This has occurred throughout history, but when actual statistics from recent wars are presented, the extent of the atrocity is overwhelming. In the war in Bosnia and Herzegovina, between 30,000 and 50,000 women were raped (44). In Bangladesh's 1971 war for independence, from 250,000 to 400,000 women were raped, producing approximately 25,000 pregnancies (45). Around this same number, but perhaps as many as half a million women, were raped during the 1994 genocide in Rwanda (46).

These statistics are sobering and difficult even to read, but acknowledging these terrible trends is the first step in stopping them. We must support our women because the women in our lives are forever supporting us. Mothers are always in the process of raising the next generation of the world's children, both boys and girls. Moreover, and contrary to popular belief, women are often the primary economic contributors to the family, especially in cases of single parenthood and divorce in the developed world, polygamy in Africa, and widowhood in South Asia (47). Women have been shown to spend a larger percentage of their income than men directly on the family's children (48). Yet, with dramatically less earning power and less ownership of land and resources, women's ability to care for children is handicapped. Organizations such as the Global Fund for Women, UNICEF, CARE, Womankind Worldwide, Women for Women International, and UNIFEM (United Nations Development Fund for Women) are powerful international forces that are turning many lurid statistics into encouraging ones.

In the wealthier nations, we can raise our girls to believe that they can and will be the leaders of the future. We should encourage them to stand out, speak up, and make their presence known at every level – from the local to the international. Women in the developed world have immense power compared to their counterparts in still developing nations, so their full engagement in this shift is absolutely critical to the planet's well-being and to the rise of women the world over.

The Power of Giving

- George C. Marshall, 1945, addressing Harvard University about the "Marshall Plan" for Europe's recovery from WWII.

The Fourth Way to Save the Planet: Give

Donate money or time to non-governmental organizations (NGOs) that focus on helping the developing world (several are listed in this chapter) or those who need help even within wealthy countries. This bridges the global gap between rich and poor by allowing resources to flow from the "haves" to the "have-nots." It is the best way to directly help the one-fourth of the world that is starving, without basic human rights, and dying by the thousands every day. Your giving also helps impoverished countries to develop economically by becoming more self-sufficient and sustainably productive. With better options for income in these nations, the lure of deforestation, animal poaching, or entering the drug or sex trades steadily diminishes. These harmful choices are simply examples of desperately poor people trying to survive by supplying first-world consumer demand. NGOs are critical because they take action, even when it is deemed politically unsavory or economically imprudent for national governments to do so. Moreover, several NGOs help to prosecute human rights abuses and war crimes, both of which show humanity's darkest side.

Didier Drogba, a striker for England's Chelsea Football Club, pledged to donate all of his endorsement earnings to build hospitals in his native Cote d'Ivoire. Malalai Joya is a young woman who defied the Taliban by earning a seat in Afghanistan's Parliament and starting underground schools to educate girls, while Elon Musk has shared his Tesla electric car battery patents with the public in order to spur the zero-emission transportation revolution (1).

Powerful, progressive, and magnanimous individuals are a critical part of the equation for the continuing evolution of this planet. Any individual has the power to uplift others. Some uplift a friend or spouse. Some uplift a classroom or a household. The will of a good quarterback can inspire a team to a victory, while the powerful spirit of a good preacher can lift a whole community. Individuals are needed and called upon at all levels of leadership and inspiration. Presidents and other national-scale leaders have innumerable times changed the course of their people's vision, focus, morale, or even their history. And there have been a few individuals who exhibited the power to uplift the entire world. We all know their names.

The power of individuals to uplift is mighty, and one way that they do this is through giving money – whether they are billionaires or bellboys. The Guggenheims, John D. Rockefeller III, and Andrew Carnegie financially supported everything from aviation and space rocketry to penicillin and guaranteed pensions for teachers. Victor Pinchuk, Ukranian millionaire, personally funded his nation's first grand-scale contemporary art center, its first private chamber orchestra, as well as a nationally televised concert with Elton John to promote AIDS awareness. On the other side of the giving coin is the March of Dimes, which was funded by the pocket change of literally millions of donors and resulted in the first polio vaccine (2). In addition, half of all hospital beds, 95% of all orchestras, and 60% of all social service organizations are funded by private individuals (3).

The United States has the most generous citizens in the world, in that they donate a much larger percentage of their GDP than the denizens of any other country. In 2014, American individuals, foundations, and corporations made donations totaling

$358 billion, a full $258 billion of which was made by individuals alone (4). Author Claire Gaudiani suggests that Americans are not generous because they are rich – rather, that they are rich because they are generous (5). That is, philanthropy throughout the generations in this country has largely been directed beyond immediate aid and toward investing in our human and infrastructural capital. For instance, private donations sent many prominent Americans to college, such as Ralph Waldo Emerson, Alice Walker, Oprah Winfrey, Itzhak Perlman, and Bill Clinton. These people all went on to considerably enrich the lives of both Americans and citizens of the globe.

Many leaders and persons who uplift do so through action rather than financial donation. Often a tragedy or tragic era provides the opportunity for a true leader or hero to rise up. The Nazi reign in Europe and the era of slavery in the U.S. produced heroes such as Arthur Schindler and Elie Weisel, and Harriet Tubman and Frederick Douglass, respectively. In fact, noting the geographic source of historical "heroes" leads us to the most poignant sites of suffering. Mohandas Gandhi, Nelson Mandela, and Stephen Biko all originally fought for minority rights in South Africa, a hyper-segregated and highly discriminative country at the time. Martin Luther King, Jr., Malcolm X, and Rosa Parks pushed for the civil rights of American Blacks in the separate but still unequal United States of the 1960s.

Today we see prominent figures such as Oprah Winfrey, Bono, Al Gore, Michael Moore, and Senator Bernie Sanders who are changing the way we think and countering many widely accepted beliefs. What does their prominence say about the current social climate in this country? What are they fighting against? Michael Moore is very controversial because he pushes hard for governmental and public policy transparency. Bernie Sanders is the first politician to advocate for political and corporate transparency on such a grand and public scale. The popularity of Sanders' campaign and Moore's documentaries are a testament to how shrouded and clandestine the operations of our government have been in recent decades.

Some altruists are fighting – and winning – battles that most of us are not even aware of. Aung San Suu Kyi has tirelessly defended democracy within dictatorial Myanmar for the majority of her life. While separated from her family under house arrest in Myanmar for over fourteen years, she managed to be elected prime minister and be awarded the 1991 Nobel Peace Prize. In India, Dr. Perumalsamy Namperumalsamy's patient list is even longer than his name. His eye-care hospitals have performed 3.6 million cataracts surgeries, giving sight to the previously blind (6). And South Africa's Elon Musk, mentioned above, is both a NASA rocket scientist and a green pioneer. He designed the all-electric Tesla sports car and helped to create Solar City, the largest residential provider of solar power in the U.S

Specific events can also elicit and necessitate new ways of helping and interacting with each other. The Hurricane Katrina and September 11 tragedies are such examples here in the U.S. These disasters were so large in scale that no individual, organization, or government could handle the care, reparations and recovery alone. We necessarily had to *collaborate* in order to significantly help. Organizations public and private, profit and non-profit, governmental and individual, all came together to begin to repair our torn cities of New York and New Orleans. This showed us a precedent for how we must handle our nation and our world in the future…together. This topic is elucidated by *Collaborative Philanthropies* author Elwood Hopkins.

There are actually over 2,000 U.S. corporations with foundations that are focused on philanthropic giving. According to Jacquelyn Smith's July 2013, *Forbes* article, "America's Most Generous Corporations," Target and Bank of America both gave away over 3% of their pre-tax profits, which is about triple the national average and close to $150 million in donations for each company (7), while ten total U.S. corporations gave between $140 million and $500 million each in donations in 2012.

In many aspects of global philanthropy, from disaster relief to eradicating poverty, benevolent organizations have begun to take the lead where national governments have waned in their eagerness to help. Many governments are still engrossed in the lure of territorial and financial conquest, and strategic political interests often mitigates a nation's philanthropy. So while prominent national governments are otherwise occupied, powerful nongovernmental organizations (NGOs) have stepped up and taken it upon themselves to intervene and offer help.

These groups can range in size and scope from a local after-school program for at-risk kids to Amnesty International with almost three million members in 150 countries. The attention and active care that NGOs offer usually centers on a few archetypal themes:

- **human rights** (Human Rights Watch, Amnesty International)
- **animals and the environment** (Greenpeace, World Wildlife Fund, The Humane Society, Sierra Club, Rainforest Action Network)
- **emergency relief/aid** (OXFAM, Red Cross, Salvation Army)

- **developing the third world** (UNESCO, Grameen Bank, Habitat for Humanity, Clinton Global Initiative, World Bank)
- **women's issues** (CARE, Women for Women International, UNICEF, Global Fund for Women)
- **promotion of peace** (Peace Action, The United Nations).

These are just a few examples, but there are literally thousands more. In fact, by 2004, there were nearly 6,600 non-governmental organizations in existence (8). These groups have the added task of learning how to suffuse their altruism into nations around the world in culturally appropriate ways.

A great example of this comes from an acquaintance of mine who went to India in the 1980s in order to research family planning and population control strategies in rural communities. He came upon one farmer's humble abode, surrounded by a barely standing fence on a remote dirt road in northern India. In his best Hindi, my friend greeted the man, described the regional benefits of birth control, and after conveying their utility, left him with about fifty condoms. Returning to the same house about a month later to check on the farmer's progress, my friend immediately saw that all of the condoms had been used, but not exactly as he had hoped. One condom had been carefully unrolled over each fencepost in the front of the house as a symbolic shield against the arrival of new children! The language barrier in this simple interaction had clearly proven to be a larger hurdle than anticipated.

This is an excellent demonstration of how well-funded policies need adept, grassroots implementation in thousands of locations across the world in order to be successful. National governments provide large sums of international aid, to their credit, yet it is often unequally distributed, embezzled by local rulers, or spent on programs that simply don't synergize well with the local culture.

In the Los Angeles area, my students at California State University, Northridge and my sister Stephanie's students at El Camino College, each gave one dollar to an organization called Kiva.org, a website that connects developing world residents in need of microloans with first world donors. In our one-semester trial, we sent around $350 to six microloan recipients in Tanzania, Nicaragua, Peru, Cambodia, Bolivia, and Kenya. Those monetary amounts may not sound sizeable to most of us, but they can make a world of difference. Even if you are a family of four that earns a combined $50,000 a year, you are a wealthy potential benefactor from the perspective of the world's one billion people living in abject poverty. In the words of *The Story of Stuff* author Annie Leonard, "We have a shortage of sharing," not a shortage of money or prosperity.

With a little more power in their checkbooks, there have been many ultra-wealthy families and throughout this country's and this globe's history have had a profound benevolent impact, from the Medecis of Renaissance Italy to the Guggenheims, McLeods, Fords, Rockefellers, Packards, Carnegies, and Kelloggs of 20th century America. Noteworthy donors in the 21st century are Gordon and Betty Moore who have given $7 billion to environmental conservation, Michael and Susan Dell who gave $1 billion to children's health and education, and Alfred Mann, who has given over $800 million for biomedical research.

A few outstanding individuals today have not only the money but the broad influence to coalesce real change in the world: Ted Turner, Bill Gates, Al Gore, and Oprah Winfrey. The philanthropy of Ted Turner in this century is, in short, amazing. He is magnanimous, very outspoken, and always quick to smile.

Christine Amanpour, who joined Turner's news station, CNN, in 1983, said "The idea of 24-hour news and global news is his creation. That's changed the world… (and) changed people's relations with their governments. It's meant that governments can no longer crack down with impunity on protests" (9). Yet Turner's service to society goes much further than that. His commitment to global peace is so great that in 1997, Ted Turner walked into United Nation's Secretary Kofi Anan's office and said "I'm going to give you a billion dollars," which he proceeded to do, with a $100 million donation each year for ten years (10).

He is also a tireless defender of environmental issues. In 2001 alone, the Turner Foundation gave almost $70 million to environmental causes, while Mr. Turner invests heavily in renewable energy projects (11)(12). Turner also publicly urged other American billionaires to "loosen up their wads" which helped to jolt Bill Gates into a philanthropic state. Eventually Gates donated $25 billion, principally toward world health and the population explosion.

Al Gore is known for being the former Vice President and was very nearly put into office as the President of the United States. Yet at his core he is a defender of the environment, and he earned a Nobel Peace Prize while furthering that mission. Beyond just a galvanizing movie, Gore's documentary, *An Inconvenient Truth,* is a strong admonishment to those who play a part in the trashing of our global environment and a universal call to duty for all to help heal it.

149

The changes that these visionary leaders bring about allow us to see that ideas and visions stimulate the confluence of people to fulfill a larger goal and new realities. Stanford University economist Paul Romer put forth the idea that an economy is founded on ideas rather than on tangible things (13). Those with good ideas are looking for the money to actualize their visions, while the wealthy are searching for deserving, ambitious individuals whom they can support. This union is what makes philanthropy so essential to the progress of a society.

Oprah Winfrey went to college on the donation of a private individual, and now her ideas and presence uplift millions of people. Certainly if anyone has gone from meager beginnings to fame, wealth, and altruism, it is Oprah. She began as a poor girl from the segregated South and went on to become, in the words of CNN and Time.com "arguably the world's most powerful woman." *Business Week* named her the greatest black philanthropist in U.S. history, and *Time* magazine cited her as one of only four people who have shaped both the 20th and 21st centuries. But what Oprah gives to the world goes beyond money or celebrity or any specific cause – she is simply a powerful loving presence. Amidst this era's barrages of negative news and propagation of fear of other countries, religions, and even of our next door neighbor, Oprah goes against that tide and encourages us to expect and highlight the good in each other and in the world.

To date, Oprah's Angel Network has raised over $70 million. In 2005 she gave away $250 million of her own money, $10 million of that to the Katrina relief effort (14). She has built a girls' school in South Africa and she spent $7 million putting 100 black men through college (15). The March 22, 2002 edition of *Christianity Today* called Ms. Winfrey "The Church of 'O,' a post-modern priestess – an icon of church-free spirituality." Very simply, it just feels good to wake up and know that Oprah is in the world, and that she's up to something good.

To conclude this idea of uplifting someone that they might uplift others in the future, a story about two young British boys may prove very encouraging. A wealthy family lived on a large 19th century English estate, and the estate grounds and home were tended to by a man, his wife and their children. The two families had sons of similar age and the boys would regularly play together. Despite not being able to swim, one day the wealthy boy jumped into the family pond, and immediately began to struggle to stay afloat. The other boy eventually saw this struggle and rushed in to save the young heir from drowning. The parents were so thankful that they said to the servant father that they would fulfill any one request that he had, no matter how large. Having a strong belief in the importance of education, he immediately said, "Send my son to medical school."

The son of the estate-owning family eventually grew up to be Winston Churchill, and he led his entire nation to victory in World War II. One day during the early 1940s, in the thrust of the war, Winston drew ill. Quite fortuitously, penicillin had just been discovered by Alexander Fleming, a British doctor and medical researcher. Doctor Fleming himself was summoned to Mr. Churchill's side to administer the shot and assess his health. A few days later the doctor returned to find Winston up and about and healthy. At the wizened doctor's approach, Winston leaned close and whispered "That's the second time you've saved my life, Dr. Fleming."

We never know when our donation of love or money or support will be the springboard to another's greatness. Nor can we perhaps imagine what magnificence will be unleashed when we do so and how it will affect, or even save, our own life. So as individuals, communities, and nations, who can we raise up now that will in turn uplift us in the future? Who among us is so gifted that they will change the way we live and think, if only we give them the start they need? What hero is waiting for your gift, your attention, your love? Are you the next great benefactor, or are you the hero who waits to bloom? Either way, now is the time to share your gifts with the world.

Living More Efficiently

"Nothing will benefit human health and increase chances for survival of life on Earth as much as the evolution to a vegetarian diet."

- Albert Einstein

"Living in this world and not being an environmentalist is like living on a boat and not having the skills of a sailor."

- Gregory J. Schwartz

The Fifth Way to Save the Planet: Live More Efficiently

In the West, indulgent consumption is at the root of our biggest problems. Trash production, wasting food, and overuse of energy are pervasive vices, and these are all centered at home. The average American family uses twice the energy of a family in Europe, four times as much energy as a family in China, and eight times as much as a family in India. Moreover, domestic water consumption per household in the U.S. is 145 gallons per day, compared to 72 gallons in France and 8 gallons in Nigeria (1). Americans also consume the most gasoline and food on the planet. An earnest commitment to conservation and more efficient living within the most wasteful countries is of the highest importance and very attainable. Unbridled consumption without responsibility is simply unsustainable since we are already over-burdening the carrying capacity of the Earth and its resources. Our consumption, when focused wisely, can actually be a powerful solution, in that it funds industries and companies that are moving the globe in the right direction.

I had a dream the other night that I was hungry but I found there was no food in my cupboards or refrigerator. Then I went to the grocery store and saw that the shelves were completely bare. The sinking realization came over me that there was no food to be found in my entire city of Los Angeles. Day after day in this excruciatingly long dream, I had to watch my wife and child, as well as my neighbors, starving to death in front of my eyes. Other essentials were also hard to come by. Our only source of water was a polluted river about two miles from our house. Since everyone was sharing this river, even for laundry and bathing, drinking from it was ill advised, but it was unfortunately our only choice. Thousands of people in the city died every day, but still nothing changed and no help came. I cannot describe the unshakeable helplessness that I felt.

The one curious twist in the dream was that we still could watch television. Each day, our predicament became harder to bear as we sat and watched news and shows from around the world picturing people living in such abundance and luxury. They looked so happy and carefree. I wondered how they could live like that while knowing what we were experiencing in L.A.

"Some care, and they do help," said my next-door neighbor, "but most don't. That's just the way it is."

The most frightening part of my dream was that when I awakened, it was real. Not for me, but for 800 million people on the planet, this nightmare is their daily life. If you live in a wealthy nation, even if you don't want it, you have a small part of the responsibility to make life better for those who are so terribly suffering elsewhere on the planet. A great place to start is to choose one or two of the several ways to save the planet listed in this book, and take action on them consistently. This small change – in just one person's life – will have ripple effects that positively affect the entire globe. No one needs to excessively abuse our resources, nor should anyone perish from lack of them. Below, I discuss how much water, energy, and food is wasted in U.S. households, and I show how managing these resources better will improve both our health and our finances.

When astronauts orbit the Earth, there are a few human-built structures that are large enough to be visible from outer space including the Egyptian pyramids, the Great Wall of China, and the Fresh Kills Landfill on the southern edge of New York City (2). That is, from a distance, what is now notable about this planet is the sheer accumulation of waste. Specifically, residents of the United States generate 1.5 billion pounds of trash *per day*. Consumption is king in the wealthy nations of the world. It is the root of our biggest environmental, financial, and health-related problems, and it also has the power to be the source of countless solutions.

Citizens of most of Europe, Canada, Japan, New Zealand, Australia, oil producing nations of the Middle East, and the United States consume food, water, and energy at exorbitant rates compared to poorer nations. Daily, the average American home uses twenty times the water and nearly ten times the energy that is used in most households in Africa. Our buying and usage habits have created a global environmental crisis both directly, by burning coal for electricity and gasoline to drive our cars, and indirectly, by buying products that necessitate deforestation such as beef, paper products, and packaged foods (palm oil).

In addition, especially in America, our fixation on food is a significant contributor to very high cancer, diabetes, and obesity rates. The powerful thing about our copious consumption is that it wields strong influence over markets, industries, resource supplies, and our own health – for good or for bad. Say, for instance, organic yogurt becomes the new craze. Instantly, there is increased demand for organic cattle feed, tons of pesticides are *not* sprayed into our air, thousands of cows are spared bovine growth hormones, and we all get a healthier end-product. We vote with our dollars in wealthy nations, and by buying environmentally friendly foods and products, we effectively choose which companies and practices flourish or flounder.

FOOD

We will begin with everyone's favorite topic: food. It may be surprising to know that each of the following people – President Bill Clinton, Leonardo Da Vinci, Pamela Anderson, Rosa Parks, Prince, NASCAR driver Andy Lally, Albert Einstein, Mike Tyson, Supermodel Christy Turlington, three of the four Beatles, Benjamin Franklin, and even fictional cartoon character Lisa Simpson – are all vegetarians (or were while they were alive). Yet fewer Americans are vegetarian (3%) than the citizens of nearly any other country on Earth, for example Italy (8%), and India (45%). I do not suggest that we all need to be vegetarians, simply that it is helpful to understand exactly how eating less meat enhances our physical health and the health of the planet.

By far, the worst culprit of all, in terms of your health and the health of the planet, is beef. Beef is a staple in the American and European diets, and increasingly so in Asia and among the *nouveau riche* worldwide. Americans eat about sixty pounds of beef per person per year; Argentines eat over twice that amount, while European consumption ranges widely from twenty to sixty-five pounds per year (3)(4). This is significant because approximately 40% of current deforestation can be attributed to clearing land for cattle grazing or for growing soybeans which will be fed to livestock (5). Moreover, World Bank environmental advisor, Robert Goodland, has shown that the global livestock industry is responsible for up to half of greenhouse gas emissions worldwide! (6). This means that eating meat (beef being the most extreme example) is estimated to be the leading cause of deforestation *and* climate change.

What's more, few people know that over one-third of the world's grain harvest is fed to livestock, including over 70% of the grain harvested in the United States (7). Enough grain is produced globally to provide each human with 3,500 calories per day (8). Yet, when grain calories are eaten by an animal, the total calories available to human consumption declines by 90% because the animal burns these calories over its lifetime (9). What this means is, if we feed our grains to people rather than animals, we will have much more food to go around.

Another resource that meat – and beef in particular – gobbles up is water. Beef has the highest water footprint of any food, and other meats and animal products are close behind. One pound of beef requires about 1,700 gallons of water to produce, pork requires around 1,000 gallons per pound, while a pound of chicken requires approximately 600 gallons, mainly because of the giant amount of irrigation required to grow an animal's food throughout its lifetime (10). In comparison, a pound of pears needs 48 gallons of water to grow, and a pound of onions only drinks 20 gallons of water in its growing cycle (11).

On the flip side of that equation is the fact that beef consumption is directly linked to the biggest killers in the Western world: cancer and heart disease. Countless studies, including two recent ones by the National Cancer Institute and the Harvard School of Public Health, have linked the eating of beef to significantly higher rates of diabetes, cancer, and heart disease (12)(13)(14)(15). For instance, eating beef every day, rather than once a week, is associated with a 20% increase in cancer rates and over a 30% increase in heart disease rates (16). Many other quite prominent studies, including Nobel Prize-winning work, continues to prove that eating fewer animal products lowers the rates of essentially all types of cancer and heart disease (17)(18) .

When will we collectively see the writing on the wall and decide to change? Beef consumption is destroying our forests, depleting food surpluses and water supplies, warming our planet, and diseasing and killing our bodies. Other meats, such as chicken and pork, are measurably less harmful – and are better choices – but still quite significant contributors to these problems. Westerners don't need to be vegetarians; all that is necessary is that we *temper* our consumption of meat in the awareness of how much good it will do the planet and our bodies. In the words of Barry Popkin, director of the obesity center at the University of North Carolina, Chapel Hill, "It's a lot of deaths you save if you go from eating a Whopper once a day to once a week instead."

Vandana Shiva, author of *Stolen Harvest*, points to the specific role of fast-food chains in this scenario:

"Junk-food chains, including KFC and Pizza Hut, are under attack from major environmental groups in the United States and other developed countries because of their environmental impact. Intensive breeding of livestock and poultry for such restaurants leads to deforestation, land degradation, and contamination of water sources and other natural resources. For every pound of red meat, poultry, eggs, and milk produced, farm fields lose about five pounds of irreplaceable top soil. The water necessary for meat breeding comes to about 190 gallons per animal per day, or ten times what a normal Indian family is supposed to use in one day, if it gets water at all" (19).

A broader question to be addressed is that we Americans are getting fatter. About 65% of Americans are overweight, while a full one-third are clinically obese, and that figure includes children. In Europe, the total percentage overweight is usually between thirty and forty percent of the population, while obesity rates normally hover between ten and twenty percent. Numbers in Asia and Africa are much lower, yet rising, especially in wealthy urban settings. The great paradox is that we eat so much in the U.S. that it is killing us, while elsewhere on this same planet 100,000 people die daily from starvation or starvation-related conditions (20).

Obesity costs the U.S. health care system between $200 billion and $340 billion annually, depending on how totals are generated (21). Yet, based on estimates from USAID (United States agency for international development), UNFAO (United Nations Food and Agriculture Organization), and the World Food Programme, it will only cost between five and six billion dollars per year to provide one daily meal to the one billion undernourished people on the planet right now (22). Clearly the resources are available to correct this imbalance. If we ate less in the U.S. and saved 20% of our annual health costs related to obesity – conservatively, $40 billion a year – that would be enough to sustain all of the hungry people on the planet indefinitely. Curbing other unhealthy habits, like smoking, could help as well. $10 billion is spent in the U.S. every year on advertising for cigarettes alone (23).

This issue of dealing with food more efficiently has other layers as well. The American Association for the Advancement of Science states that 78% of the world's malnourished children live inside countries which actually have food *surpluses* (24). Eleven countries in Sub-Saharan Africa are net food exporters while over 200 million people in that region are drastically under-nourished (25).

160

Even during the severe droughts of the late 70s and early 80s, food was exported from the most ravaged countries in the desertified Sahel region of Africa. In India in 1995, again over 200 million people were essentially starving, yet the nation exported $625 million worth of wheat and flour, and $1.3 billion worth of rice (26).

What's going on is that these countries are determined to earn foreign capital, achieve a favorable balance of trade, and get out of debt, so selling food on the international market is more attractive than feeding it to their own people. This approach is condoned by loan contingencies imposed upon these nations. These policies force destitute nations to cut off services and funding to their own underserved citizenry in favor of producing cash crops and manufactured products for export. This mimics the exploitative tactics utilized by colonial powers in the 18th and 19th centuries.

Amidst this global fight against hunger, one unlikely factor – school lunches – are playing a huge role. George McGovern, a one-time candidate for U.S. President, was appointed by President John F. Kennedy in 1961 to head the U.S. Food for Peace Program. Then and now, Mr. McGovern sees school lunches as critical to the development of the poorest nations. Malnourished children do not have the energy or means to attend school and succeed. A free school lunch has been shown to dramatically increase school attendance and academic performance (27). This tackles two huge problems – illiteracy and malnutrition – at the same time, and reinforces the truth that they are intimately tied together. In fact, the first two of eight Millennium Development goals, created at a special session of the UN in 2000, are to "Eradicate hunger and extreme poverty" and "Achieve universal primary education" by the year 2015.

161

WATER

Unfortunately, children who live in extreme poverty face more challenges than just hunger. Hundreds of millions of children in the developing world spend a large portion of their waking hours every day engrossed in one specific task: searching for water.

Three years ago in 2009, Jean Bosco was a fifteen-year-old boy who lived in a village in rural Rwanda. His family had a simple one-room hut, with walls made of wood slats and mud. In the dry season, Jean awoke each morning and had to walk over a mile to the nearest source of water – a murky pond – in order to fill the family's plastic 20-gallon "Jerry can" with foul-smelling water. Jean placed the heavy can on his head for the one- mile trek back home. He then repeated this trip four or five times a day, every day.

At home, the water had to be boiled – using precious firewood – in order to remove parasites and bacteria. Then the precious water was allowed to cool before it could be used for drinking or bathing. Those who couldn't spare the firewood or buy chlorine to purify the water often developed skin rashes, diarrhea, and vomiting spells from ingesting the contaminated water. In the end, Jean's days were very simply and monotonously filled with carrying water to and fro, which had another very unfortunate side effect: he often could not attend school.

Then one day in 2009, a group called *Charity: Water* built a well in Jean's village, funded by $5,000 of private donations. The entire village gathered around and erupted in joyful shouting as the first pure, clean water poured out of the newly cemented well. The children played and splashed in the abundant clear water, and you could see the stress on the parents' faces be replaced by jubilation and relief. No more daily trekking by women and children to the distant water source. No more missing school just to collect water. Nearly identical stories, not all with happy endings, are happening all over Africa, India, and central America as water becomes an ever more critical resource.

Wise management of water is more immediate and essential than most of us realize. The combination of two factors – the skyrocketing global population and global warming – are stretching the planet's water resources so thin that massive collective changes in how we use this precious resource will soon be forthcoming.

The World Health Organization estimates that five million people die each year from ingesting contaminated or heavily polluted water. By and large, this is not because they unknowingly ingest unhealthy water, but because they have no other choice but to drink contaminated water.

Over the centuries, societies have risen and fallen because of their access to and skillful management of water. Rome and Angkor Wat in Cambodia, thought to be the first two cities on Earth to reach one million inhabitants, both had famed and elaborate aqueduct systems. And for all of the cultures that plentiful water has fueled, extreme drought has extinguished just as many. Yet in many industrialized societies, an illusion is cultivated of an unlimited supply of water and other resources.

I had my college students fill out written surveys about their water usage and opinions and some of the results were shocking. While the average shower length was 11 minutes, many students' daily showers were from 30 minutes to one full hour! And this is in the midst of California's worst drought in a half century.

As I reported in the introduction to this chapter, the average U.S. household uses 145 gallons of water per day, while in Spain the average is 75 gallons per day, and in Ethiopia it is 5 gallons per day (28). It's important to remember that the amount of water on the planet, though infinitely recyclable, is precisely finite. Only 3% of the water on earth is fresh water, and most of that is frozen in glaciers and in the ice fields of Greenland and Antarctica. So in the end, less than 1% of the water on Earth is accessible for human survival, and that comes from precipitation or groundwater.

We all rely on the hydrologic cycle to bring water to us. The problem is, we are extracting water from rivers and groundwater faster than precipitation can replenish them. Several rivers no longer even reach the sea, including the formerly mighty Colorado River which once carved the Grand Canyon. The Aral Sea, previously the fourth-largest lake on the planet, is now totally gone due to water extraction for irrigation by regional farmers. Also, global warming is dramatically accelerating glacial melting, which is depleting an important and steady source of fresh water.

Many desert communities get as much as 70% of their fresh water supply from groundwater, especially in drought years. Las Vegas, Nevada and Palm Springs, California are among them (29). The California cities of Barstow, Banning, and Indio glean 100% of their fresh water from groundwater reserves (30). If too much water is withdrawn at rates faster than the natural "recharge rate," then land subsidences can happen where giant sections of land simply sink several feet. This has been happening in California's San Joaquin Valley since the 70s when farmers were withdrawing as much as 48 billion gallons (150,000 acre feet) of water per day (31).

In 1977, literally one-half of this gigantic valley sank approximately one foot (32), and several small sections sank over fifteen feet. These land subsidences continue today because California still gets over one-third of its total fresh water from groundwater pumping. If we keep tapping these sources, desert plant roots can no longer reach the water table during drought, and pumping deeper and deeper becomes exorbitantly expensive, so massive desert communities will have to be abandoned.

When we over-allocate river water and continually increase the amount siphoned off, it has a huge effect on fish and aquatic populations, which of course we rely on for food. Less than half of the original river water flow from the Sierra Nevada Mountains now reaches the San Francisco Bay. Its waters are tapped by cities as far away as Los Angeles, 400 miles to the south.

Faced with national water shortages in 2010, then president of Brazil, Luiz da Silva, urged his citizens to urinate in the shower, saving millions of toilet flushes per day. Up to one-fourth of the world's countries' water resources are already stressed, and this is predicted get much worse as populations soar. Millions of developing-world residents are forced to pay private distributors handsomely to acquire clean water, often up to one-third of their total income.

The easiest way to save water is to change your diet to be more plant-based. Consider this: eating a pound of beef uses the same amount of water as showering for 13 hours! Another stat that many of us don't know is that half of domestic water consumption actually happens outside – mostly to water lawns and plants. Replacing a lawn with vegetation that requires little water such as succulent plants, ivy, or low shrubs saves huge amounts of water and money annually. Even eating organic foods is an indirect way of saving water, because high-quality soils on organic farms retain more water than degraded conventional soils (33).

And let's not forget the direct link between water and energy. It requires water to make energy and it requires energy to transport water. Hundreds of gallons of water are used in coal, natural gas, and nuclear-energy production facilities to produce each megawatt hour of electricity (34). Palo Verde, the largest nuclear plant in the U.S., uses 20 billion gallons of fresh water every year to cool its reactors. On the flip side, California's largest consumer of electricity is the pumping of water through its extensive pipelines and canals to supply dry central and southern California with water.

GASOLINE

In the United States, we love our big SUVs and our fast sports cars. Our horsepower fixation has been cultivated by advertisements that attempt to connect our car's power to our personal power. Highlighting the moment when we might explode down an empty woodland highway, these advertisements forget to mention that the other 99% of our driving time, that excessive and unnecessary horsepower will simply be guzzling gas as we slowly navigate urban traffic. So I guess I'll have to be the "buzz-kill" parent in the room and say this: the notion that we all need a 300-horsepower sports car or big sport-utility vehicle in order to express and exert our dominance and uniqueness is both silly and irresponsible.

More deceptive is the perceived need for ultra-powerful work trucks. The overwhelming majority of trucks and SUVs sold never haul heavy equipment or go off-roading, as depicted in commercials. Yet these monstrous vehicles are usually fully equipped to do so. The proud owner of a 2010 Ram 1500 truck can roar down the street to go pick up bread at the market with the "security" and power of 400 horses under the hood. The 2002 model of the same truck had only 245 horsepower.

This insidious escalation of horsepower gradually gets the public accustomed to inflated horsepower numbers, not to mention giant-sized trucks and SUVs, so that anything less seems inadequate. All the while, our vehicles get larger, heavier, and use wider tires, all of which equate to lower gas mileage.

Just for some perspective, Henry Ford's original Model T was equipped with a four-cylinder, twenty-horsepower engine, and the 1966 Volkswagen Beetle had only forty horsepower. These are two of the best-selling cars of all time and they were quite capable of moving people from point A to point B.

For the true speed lover and car enthusiast, there is actually one positive loophole where performance and sustainability come together: electric cars. Contrary to popular perception, electric-car motors are faster than gasoline engines. Because power is generated by the repulsion of positive and negative electrical forces, electric motors give cars astonishingly high torque, resulting in exceptional zero-to-sixty times. One all-electric car on the market right now is the Tesla Model S P100D. It gets almost 300 miles to one charge, goes zero-to-sixty in 2.4 seconds, and produces no emissions. That makes it one of the fastest production cars in history. Just for comparison, the 2016 McLaren 570S goes 0-60 in 3.1 seconds, and the Ferrari 488 GTB does it in 3.0. And by the way, these two cars cost two or three times as much as the Tesla.

If that didn't sell you, then this will: to fully charge an electric car costs about $10! That means that you can go 300 miles in the new Tesla Model S for ten measly dollars. That's like paying 70 cents a gallon for gasoline. Sounds like a no-brainer. What's more, Tesla has placed hundreds of rapid superchargers on U.S. highways which provide free charging for Tesla owners for life. Now, I can't be held accountable if hundreds of wheezing, gas-guzzling cars are abandoned on the sides of American roads as their owners march straight to a Tesla dealer after reading this paragraph. Tesla is one of a few companies that are proving that when electric cars finally get a foothold in the market, they will comprise a revolution in eco-friendly, high-performance, affordable, and chic transportation.

What surprises most people is that electric cars have been around for over a century. In fact, in the year 1900, there were already more electric cars on U.S. roads than gasoline-powered ones (35). Henry Ford's wife even drove one. But oil companies immediately saw electric vehicles as a threat and so they have consistently and very stealthily squelched every attempt at resurgence that the zero-emissions car has made. A recent such action was Texaco's mid-1990s buyout of Stan Oshinsky's high-performance batteries, which were to be used in General Motors' EV-1 all-electric cars (36).

GM, together with an oil-company coalition, also sued the state of California in 2001 when it attempted to mandate that 10% of all cars produced by auto manufacturers be totally emission-free. GM won the suit, despite the fact that a majority of Californians supported the mandate (37).

More egregious than that was the U.S. government single-handedly ushering in the era of the giant SUV truck in this country. It began with a seemingly innocuous portion of the U. S. tax code, which granted small business owners a $25,000 tax break for the purchase of a vehicle weighing over 6,000 pounds (38). Only the largest SUVs with the lowest fuel economy qualified for the cut. Yet in 2003 that deduction was raised to a shocking $100,000. Addressing then US energy secretary, Spencer Abraham, in an October 12, 2003 interview, *60 Minutes* reporter Lesley Stahl stated "…there's an encouragement for the small business person not just to stay afloat but to go buy the biggest gas guzzler there is… the 6,000 pound car… the biggest. Does that make sense? You can almost buy the whole car for the tax break." Soon after, the age of the SUV began in earnest in the U.S. and giant vehicles conspicuously began to show up on our roads as millions took advantage of this inflated tax loophole.

During this same period the maximum deduction for purchasing a hybrid car was a mere $4,000 (39). Unless a citizen were uncommonly inquisitive into the written tax code, she would not unearth this glaring incentive for Americans to turn away from environmentally friendly automobiles to the most offensive gas guzzlers available.

Whatever dismissive thought that pops into the head of the average U.S. citizen when he hears a discussion of electric cars is most likely the result of carefully calculated suppression, omission, or falsification of information about these wonderful cars. As in the case of the Tesla mentioned above, electric cars are blazingly fast, they have plenty of range, and they are virtually silent. But their two greatest virtues which place them head-and-shoulders above gasoline-powered cars

169

is that electric cars, of course, produce no emissions, and they are essentially maintenance-free.

Electric motors have only one moving part and do not require oil for lubrication, water for cooling, nor air intake for combustion. There are no fuel pumps, valves, or alternators which are common causes of breakdowns. Transmissions have only one forward gear in electric cars and hence have fewer problems than conventional ones. Electric cars should have revolutionized urban transportation over a hundred years ago, and when they fully arrive, they will do nothing less than that today. Imagine our cities with dramatically less freeway or street noise, and no smog! That reality is quite attainable – if we only know that it is possible and choose it.

TRASH

Did you happen to ever catch an episode of the MTV show called "Room Raiders?" Disgruntled girlfriends or conniving roommates would rummage through a friend's bedroom, hoping to find dirty secrets. One tactic that they'd often employ was looking through the victim's waste basket. It surprised me how much they could deduce about someone's recent behavior simply from what they'd thrown away. And this works on a larger scale, too. It sounds strange, but you can surmise quite a bit about an entire society just by digging through their garbage.

In Thailand, I once rented a scooter and followed a garbage truck around all day in order to gain better insight into what, and how much, they consumed. A few years earlier in downtown Buenos Aires, I had seen homeless mothers and their children eating their nightly meal of leftover hamburger patties thrown into the dumpster behind a McDonald's restaurant.

Another "trash experience" in Nairobi, Kenya I happened to witness by accident. Sitting in a small empty lot behind a restaurant and eating my lunch, I saw a truck filled with trash pull up and promptly dump its contents into the empty lot. Immediately, a few people peeked out from between the buildings and grabbed items from the pile that were salvageable – bike tires, a chair, a few dishes and a plate. After this, a second wave of curious pile-pickers identified and reclaimed usable materials like string, swaths of leather, and any sizeable pieces of plastic or metal.

Almost as if on cue, as the last few people left, four or five emaciated dogs crept in and gobbled up most of the uneaten food in the shrinking heap of garbage. The entire procession lasted the better part of an hour, finished off by a small flock of birds that descended on the pile and ate any remaining food. Only perhaps one-third of the original pile of trash now remained. I surmised that this sequence probably played out in exactly the same way every day. The relative poverty of the Nairobi region, no doubt, was the main incentive for such extensive reusing and recycling, but whatever the cause, conscientious management of resources to that degree was a refreshing sight.

In stark contrast to this African method of handling refuse, residents of the United States produce about 1.5 billion pounds of trash every day, and 500 billion pounds of trash per year (40). Thirty years ago, we produced half of that amount. About 65% of this garbage is simply piled up in landfills, but a surprising amount somehow ends up in our oceans.

A few decades ago, competitive sailor Charles Moore said he once sailed his yacht for days through a giant swirling mass of plastic waste the size of Texas which has since come to be called the "Great Pacific Garbage Patch." After exploring the planet's oceans for many years and finding copious plastic pollution, Moore had this to say:

"No matter where you are, there's no getting over it, no getting away from it. It's a plastic ocean now…we're putting everything in the ocean on a plastic diet." Indeed, in some regions, large percentages of dead marine life are found to have plastic in their stomachs because they ingest it thinking it is food.

Moore's "discovery" makes us necessarily reassess how much non-biodegradable plastic that we will continue to manufacture and buy. And it also forces us to acknowledge how much sheer waste that we produce as a Westernized culture.

Capitalist economies like the United States are based on ever-increasing production and consumption. Exactly how our consumption effects the environment is effectively obscured from the general public, but these ramifications are increasingly hard to ignore. Author Dorothy L. Sayers said in 1942 that "A society in which consumption has to be artificially stimulated in order to keep production going is a society founded on trash and waste, and such a society is a house built upon sand" (41). This imminent crisis is turning many heads toward the option of recycling.

Nearly all trash – 95% – is reusable or recyclable, but in the U.S. only 35% of the total garbage collected, the waste stream, is recycled or diverted to other environmentally feasible destinations (42). The UK and Greece are even worse than the U.S. in this category, but countries like Germany and the Netherlands should be commended that they recycle close to two-thirds of their trash. Small nations like Denmark, Japan, and Luxembourg choose to burn over half of their trash due to space constraints, but the heat produced is used to generate electricity.

In a San Fernando Valley neighborhood in Los Angeles, a man named "Buck" understands the inherent value of trash. He used to be a boxer until he found that he made more money and could support his kids just by recycling full-time. He drives his truck up to all of the public dumpsters in the city and simply pulls out valuable recyclables like glass, plastic, and aluminum, which make up about 25% of this country's municipal solid waste stream. Though it's not a very glamorous job, he told me that he makes between forty and sixty thousand dollars per year! So for Buck, the trash is full of cash.

When I pass a garbage truck or city dump, I don't see waste, I see energy, cash, fertilizer, and countless still useable items. This is what is in our trash, if we just take it to the right destination and allow them to convert it into these very desirable end products. For example, over half of the trash in the U.S. is made of paper and food. It was discovered that when the sixteen million tons of food thrown away every year rots, it releases methane gas which destroys the ozone layer and accelerates global warming even more quickly than carbon dioxide. One simple solution has been to separate food from the waste stream and burn the methane gas that it generates for heat energy. The conversion is termed "biomass utilization." Six Rwandan prisons have implemented a similar process whereby methane gas is siphoned off of toilet sewage and used to provide cooking fuel for prison kitchens that each feed thousands of inmates (43). This program has been successfully operated since 2001 and halves the amount of fuel wood that was formerly used in the prison system.

Only two percent of Americans are farmers, so few of us realize how important and expensive fertilizer is. But there's free fertilizer in the trash! Composting food waste and yard trimmings – allowing it to biodegrade in a hot, moist environment for a few weeks – is an excellent source of free fertilizer. When I worked at *Raw Energy* organic café in Berkeley, California, my friend named Wendell, who was homeless, came by each day to pick up the giant bag of cellulose pulp that we had generated from our juicer. He took it to the Berkeley community organic garden where the cellulose was applied directly to the soil as organic compost fertilizer. In countless cities, much of the enormous amount of biodegradable materials thrown away each year is being composted and converted into fertilizer for local farms. Worms are even sometimes used in "vermi-composting" facilities in order to transform the waste into fertilizer within twenty-four hours!

One company called "Last Chance Mercantile" in Monterey, California truly brings to life the adage that one man's trash is another man's treasure. The company grosses hundreds of thousands of dollars per year by selling items recovered from the trash such as furniture, housewares, bicycles, and clothing. A similar, yet larger, program in Berkeley called "Urban Ore" currently takes in well over one million dollars annually (44).

I always stress to my college students that we cannot continue to dig up unlimited raw materials in order to make our products and then throw away unlimited amounts of trash on the other end of this production line. Nearly every product that we use comes directly from nature. Paper comes from trees, glass is made from silica sand, and iron ore must be mined in order to make steel. Also, remaking products from materials we already have saves an enormous amount of energy. Making a new aluminum can from a recycled can requires 95% less energy than making a can from raw materials.

Many Native American tribes, the first inhabitants of North America, provided an excellent example of how to live in harmony with nature by taking only what they needed from nature and using all that they took. If a buffalo had to be killed, every part of it was used, from the meat and hide to the tendons and sinews. That shows a respect for and understanding of the environment. We can also learn from nature itself, where all minerals, organic materials, water and air on Earth have been recycled over and over for billions of years. The waste of one process – humans breathing in oxygen and exhaling carbon dioxide – becomes the building blocks of another process – plants taking in carbon dioxide and giving off oxygen. The same recycling process is evident in the cosmos with the life cycle of stars and galaxies.

I personally see it as part of a divine design that the two most abundant elements in the Earth's terrestrial crust, after oxygen, are silicon (a fundamental ingredient in glass making) and aluminum. Glass and aluminum happen to be infinitely recyclable substances. They never lose their structural integrity, as opposed to paper or plastic, which can only be recycled a handful of times. It is as if these materials were placed right at our feet so we would assuredly use them and benefit from their sustainable utility.

Living more efficiently overall allows the industrialized world to shift from a disposable lifestyle to a sustainable lifestyle. As the Western world lives now, our indulgence is slowly crippling the environment and causing billions of others to go without. We can turn this trend around by living conscientiously and using the power of our dollars and our consumption to support responsible companies that are moving us in the right direction. And our politicians have an obligation as well to use their wisdom to responsibly guide society, and not simply play accomplice to the profit motives of giant corporations (45). We are all stewards of the Earth who will pass it on to future generations. The more we realize this and accept this role, the more rapidly our biggest problems will be solved.

The Gift of Tragedy

Visions of a Bold and Inevitable Future
for the United States and the World

"History is a race between education and catastrophe."

- H.G. Wells

Today on this Earth, 15,000 people will starve to death. Hundreds of young girls will be forced into the sex trade, 30,000 acres of forest will be cut down, and a few hundred thousand members of the U.S. military will arise and patrol a foreign country.

Most of us in the Western world have a vague understanding of these realities, but it is often very easy for us to continue life as usual – picking out tile for the new bathroom, rounding our triceps at the gym, livestreaming our favorite TV drama series – all while others beseech the heavens for a bag of rice or a life-saving penicillin shot for their child.

And so sometimes we need a wake-up call to return our focus to what is essential in this life and on this Earth. Our parents and grandparents got a few doozies – two world wars, the largest ever stock market crash, war-time and experimental atomic bomb detonations, and nuclear meltdowns like Chernobyl. But maybe those wake-up calls are too distant to still affect most of us who are not awake. (Un)luckily, we are still receiving plenty of these jarring wake-ups of late:

9/11
The 2004 Tsunami in Asia
Hurricane Katrina in 2005
The 2009 global financial crisis
The 2010 Haiti and Chile earthquakes
The 2010 BP "Deepwater Horizon" oil spill in the Gulf of Mexico
The 2011 Fukushima nuclear meltdown
The Syrian refugee crisis
Political upheaval in the United States

These huge and jarring events come along and they shake us to our core – for the very purpose of reminding us *of* our core – those we love, our health, and the health of our home, this planet. The messages of 9/11 and of the tsunami, while apparent immediately, are even more clear in retrospect. The tragedy of 9/11 evoked the greatest show of national unity and compassion for fellow Americans that many of us have ever witnessed. It also had the potential to illuminate the implications of our government's activities in the Middle East, but this realization, en masse, was not actualized.

The tsunami, because its victims were locals as well as tourists from all over the world, had the amazing effect of creating an instant global community. All of us were hurt, all of us were affected, all of us were helping. It was an astonishing equalizer and it provided an effective experience of our interconnectedness. It also served to bring an outpouring of help, resources, and Western attention onto some of the most destitute parts of the world – namely, Indonesia and India.

In a larger sense, and perhaps in some benefit to the world, the Haiti earthquake of 2010 jarred us enough to cut through our cultural myopia and daily routines and let us see how bad conditions really are, even so close to a wealthy nation like the U.S. Surprising to many who watched the devastation on television was that even before the quake, Haiti was in dire straits and was the poorest country in the western hemisphere. We were all implored to sit and gaze upon the despair of our close island neighbors, and millions were spurred to offer help in one form or another.

Disasters are an effective way for the living Earth to "communicate" with us as individuals. The Earth is a dynamic living system which displays an amazing ability to adapt and rebalance itself after destabilizing events and eras on the globe. In this way the Earth could be said to be one whole living organism, or even to have a consciousness. Empirical scientists would remark that the recent documented rise in the frequency of earthquakes is the result of increased subterranean fracking or variations in mantle convection currents, while more storms are explained by the increased ocean temperatures giving more energy to tropical low pressure systems. Metaphysical explanations may suggest that these disasters are Earth's way of rebalancing itself and of waking us up so that we may come into harmony with it.

Human-induced disasters like 9/11 could be said to arise in a similar way, in that an unacknowledged part of society, or the collective human consciousness, has asserted itself so that we must take notice and begin to come into harmony with *it*. One Saudi terrorist leader said after 9/11, "If our messages had been able to reach you through words, we wouldn't have been delivering them through planes" (1). Jarring events, both human and environmental in source, arise to bring awareness to parts of humanity which are isolated or which do not perceive themselves or their actions to be affecting the larger whole.

Hurricane Katrina jarred and affected many of us, but have we gotten the insights that it has sent us? The shock has passed but have we still not yet absorbed the inherent messages that the hurricane has provided? If any jarring event comes into your life and your response is only sadness or shock or anger or confusion, then you have not received the message, and another wake-up call is likely to come. She did. Her name, this time, was Hurricane Rita, but the message was still the same. And so, we must look to the deeper messages that Katrina and Rita offer to us. Because the only reason any "tragedy" arises is so that a greater ongoing tragedy can be brought to our attention, and stopped.

The first result and message that Katrina provided was to bring our government's focus back onto home turf. Our government, for good or bad, often spends a large portion of its energies, money, and focus on endeavors outside of this country. Fighting wars, acquiring new markets and resources, and involving ourselves in the affairs of various nations across the globe leaves less time to focus on our own people, our own cities, our own issues. Katrina reminded us of that. Also due to Katrina, many in this country have acquired a true sympathy for those in other nations who are in catastrophic, desperate situations. It is often very easy for us to get lost in our lives of entertainment and relative luxury and to passively ignore the obvious tribulations of much of the rest of the world. The hurricane gave us a visceral first-hand feeling of commonality with the struggles in the developing world, in particular the millions of dislocated peoples and refugees that we see depicted on television so often. One New Orleans woman said it best when viewing images of her city in shambles: "It looks like the third world."

Another human-induced "disaster," the global financial crisis of 2009, seems to have gotten virtually everyone's attention. For a brief moment we saw into the dicey innards of lending institutions and stock markets and how they sometimes recklessly manage or even take other people's money. I admired the presidents and members of congress of various countries who pushed for circumspect caution when delivering bail-out money to their domestic institutions. In the U.S., the financial crisis uncovered significant corruption and mismanagement and, thankfully, generated more – though not nearly enough – oversight and supervision of these oligarchic big-money players.

I had a wake-up call of my own several years ago while on a flight over central Bolivia. About twenty minutes after takeoff, one of the plane's engines failed and we immediately began to plummet toward the Earth. Losing cabin pressure, the oxygen masks dropped down and histrionics ensued. Amidst this total chaos, images of my family back home in California came into my head and I could think about nothing else. I felt utterly alone – crash landing in a plane in Bolivia, seated next to complete strangers – but I was shown in that moment what, and who, was truly important to me. The pilot eventually regained control and made a successful emergency landing.

One-time precipitous events like crash landings and plunging stock markets often serve as excellent wake-up calls, but on an everyday basis, there are ongoing global crises that demand our attention – like climate change, starvation, and the sex trade. Often we place all of our focus on what's *urgent* and little focus on what is truly *important*. Steven Covey, author of *The Seven Habits of Highly Effective People*, suggests that all actions are a combination of urgent/not urgent and important/not important. Helping someone who is having a heart attack is urgent *and* important while exercising or getting work done is not urgent but still important. Covey believes that we spend inordinate amounts of time doing things which are neither urgent nor important, such as watching television, gossiping on the phone, or indulging in other distractions. And many of these time-wasters feign urgency, such as answering a ringing phone or quenching a caffeine craving. All the while, the important things on our planet and in our lives go untended to.

But how do we get so immersed in these unimportant endeavors to the point that we need continued jarring wake-up calls in recent years on a societal level? The answer for Westerners is, simply, that we live in relative isolation and distraction . The modern American denizen has days filled with sound and fury yet sometimes devoid of global awareness and deeper significance. Each day we are flooded with entertainment and stimulation: from sugar and coffee fixes to a buffet of online streaming options and an entire apothecary of recreational drugs to 5,000-song iPods, elaborate video games for adults, and phones that connect us in real-time to the daily events of thousands of other people. This deluge can effectively nudge our attention off of any substantive national or global-level concerns.

We are also isolated from the world's problems physically, by two oceans, and ideologically, by the carefully-selected media images that give us a limited view of the world outside of our cultural bubble. And only about 15% of Americans own a passport, while that number is tripled in most European countries.

Moreover, the average European, African, or Asian resident speaks two to three languages, but most Americans, especially non-recent immigrants, speak only English. Thus, while we do live in a multi-ethnic society and speak a universal language, America's geographic and cultural dominance doesn't require that we investigate or even consider other cultures or ways of life as we go about our day. This is especially true in provincial pockets within our nation and among those who were born and raised here.

Without the daily demands of 19th century pioneer life, and with somewhat restricted awareness of the larger world's problems, we just fill our time with distraction and entertainment. Are not entertainers one of our most well-paid cohorts? I believe that America and its citizens, having amply achieved subsistence individually, and unmatched global influence nationally, simply long for a new goal. Our hearts ache in the deep subconscious awareness that there are so many problems on this Earth, so many of us suffering, and yet many of us do very little about it. This lack of purpose may literally be killing us. Without a purpose and a goal that animates us and in some way affects the world, we sink into excessive consumption, technological distraction, and meaningless entertainment. And each day that this goes on, our soul, the heart of who we are, dies a small death. And so in this developed world, the number one killer is disease of the heart, or heart disease: the symptom of an unengaged self, an unexpressed soul. Moreover, a full 20% of us are currently taking anti-depressant medication.

Some of this need is indeed finding expression in the form of magnanimous individuals and organizations which are offering help where it is most needed. The environmental movement, the push for universal human rights, and rapid disaster-relief responses are evidence of this philanthropy. Countless careers burgeon in the green economy and in the holistic sectors of business, health care, and the food industry. Yet the activities of perhaps the majority of Westerners still do not extend beyond their own microcosm, and they are often not connected to a larger social cause.

One tactic that keeps us distracted and also disconnected from other parts of the world is fear. Beginning on September 11, 2001, a shroud of fear was pulled over the American public. Rather than urging us to look into what caused 9/11, we are taught to simply fear terrorist attacks or even to fear Muslims in general. When human beings experience acute fear of an external threat, our primal "fight-or-flight" response is engaged, and we become totally focused on averting immediate danger. This response to a potential threat is natural, yet when this primal response is continually activated day after day, our attention is never allowed to settle on rational daily or domestic issues. Constant and acute fear also goads us into relinquishing many of our freedoms in the name of safety. Hence the Patriot Act.

Consumerism is also an omnipresent distraction from living out our purpose. This is true in many western cultures and increasingly in China. Television, consumerism's greatest tool, shifts our brains from an active and alert state of Beta-wave production to a much slower Alpha-wave state, clinically similar to a light hypnosis. Consistent television viewers shift to this passive, suggestible Alpha state often within a minute of turning on the tube (2). Commercials manufacture demand by hawking their wares directly into our defenseless brains. Due to marketing, packaging, and advertising, a homogenization of products is created whereby the conditions, laborers, and natural materials which came together to produce an item are very effectively obscured. This keeps Western consumers insulated from an awareness of how their purchases might be perpetuating harmful global trends. The simple act of constantly buying and consuming is a ubiquitous and powerful distraction in our society and it can keep us centered on our individual needs, and on the local, provincial scale.

Hence, broadly, through fear, consumerism, and entertainment, people in the developed world are kept distracted, numbed, over-stimulated, and yet still under-engaged. In the absence of a real goal, our desire to live lives of consequence still spills forth, and it emerges in myriad ways: stress from an imbalanced focus on money and career, diseased hearts and depressed minds from a lack of true connection and purpose in the world, and excess weight from sedentary lives. These are our national diseases, the symptoms of our lack of actualized agency, the evidence of our stalled, aching, imploding potential.

That said, hard work and productivity in the West has nonetheless generated immense prosperity over the last few centuries and pushed the world forward. Technological and industrial innovation, ingenuity, and human capital the world over allows for constant evolution and re-creation of national economies. Aviation has given way to space exploration, doctors now treat our bodies on the microbial level, and friendship groups can now stretch across oceans and continents. Societal progress, too, is moving into a new realm.

The next step for the world's wealthy nations is to shift from individual goals to collective ones and to seek progress through collaboration, rather than through competition. In a word, this depicts a state of compassion. This ideological shift will represent the arrival of the final stage of development for the industrialized world.

Virtually every powerful western society has moved through an evolution which has been based on the acquisition of money and power – first colonialism, then manufacturing, then technology, and then information and entertainment. Next and finally, because its own needs are sufficiently met, a society's goals can make the critical shift from an inward focus to an outward and compassionate focus. Nascent expressions of such benevolent societies are now observable in pockets on several continents, but especially in Europe. Northern and Western Europe display the highest quality of life on the planet, and this region also contains some of the most compassionate and environmentally aware nations on Earth.

By the late 20th century the U.S. had already achieved a good measure of global dominance financially, culturally, and politically, but its oligarchic cravings for more markets and resources ravenously marched it forward. In the past 200 years, the evolution of America's goals and collective purpose has been as follows: Independence from England . . . Manifest Destiny . . . .becoming a manufacturing powerhouse...global military domination . . . and finally cultural hegemony.

The end of this approach, however, is within sight, as evidenced by the casualties of America's over-evolution: the deaths it causes in overseas wars, its bankrupted national purse, and the diminished quality – from lack of attention – of many domestic institutions, infrastructures, and amenities. The government's sluggish response to the devastation in New Orleans is a vivid example of this.

What we crave is a totally fresh, magnanimous direction in which to channel our considerable brain-power, resources and latent energy in the West. At the same time, a huge portion of the planet's people are destitute, struggling, and beleaguered, while the natural environment is in crisis. As we in the West gradually wake up, we will start to see how the needs of the developing world as well as the environment can be intimately interwoven with our new potential benevolent purpose.

Our national pride and fulfillment would soar if we used our ingenuity and substantial resources to push for sustainable living among wealthy nations, and to help ameliorate human struggles in the poorest ones. And this is precisely what the developing world desires most – to be supported as equals, rather than subjugated, by the entities that have the power and the choice to do either one. Developing world leaders have a tall order themselves. They must work to expose corruption and eschew cultural isolation, both of which hamper international collaboration, and hence, development. Moreover, they must control their skyrocketing populations and manage the earth's precious rainforests.

Evidence of a collaborative spirit was seen in President Obama's inauguration speech back in 2008. In the following sentence, (which was likely in his own words because it does not appear in the official speech transcript) the new president conveyed a rather revolutionary sentiment:

"To all the other peoples and governments who are watching today . . . know that America is a friend of each nation, and every man, woman, and child who seeks a future of peace and dignity – and we are ready to lead once more."

In your hand, you have a guide to saving the planet with simple everyday actions, and there are always more ways to help. A consistent dose of our help and attention would heal huge portions of what ails the most destitute parts of this globe on a scale that is perhaps unimaginable. The most refreshing new direction for us, in the Western nations, will be to offer the world what we have always tried to give ourselves – the power of self-determination, opportunity for economic and social advancement, and in following, prosperity and abundance.

And for the citizens and politicians who equate compassion with weakness and who still long for the traditional, more archaic expressions of power, what bigger power rush can there be than to be at the helm of a league of wealthy, altruistic nations who choose to heal the earth's environment and usher the globe into an unprecedented level of egalitarian prosperity? We have this power in the U.S. if we work unselfishly with other nations. In every political and personal encounter, compassion is always the evidence of greatest power, while attack and avarice reek of desperation and weakness.

Americans have always been trend setters, innovators, and the hardest workers that I've ever witnessed. As an amalgam of immigrants from every country on Earth, we managed to build the globe's most powerful nation in less than 200 years. I am proud both of America's imperfect but prodigious past and its imminent benevolent future.

And now, at this critical turning point in history, the prowess and influence of the U.S. along with the Western countries reaches every corner of the globe. For this reason, the redirection of our national focus from individual goals to collective ones would generate immeasurable prosperity and unity across the globe. As the citizens and government of the United States, it is simply our choice in the coming years whether we will continue to consume without limit and support governmental and corporate aggression overseas, or if we will finally let go of the need for conquest, extend our hand to wealthy and developing nations alike, and commit to building a mutually abundant future…together.

Some Practical Suggestions for Taking Action to Save the Planet

CONVERTING TO SOLAR:

If you own your home, essentially all solar companies will now install solar panels for no money down and make your monthly payments to be less than your current electric bill. In other words, by going solar, you instantly *save* money. This option is called a solar "lease." You can also buy the panels, which does require a down payment, but monthly payments afterwards can also be similar in size to current electric bills. Then in ten years or so when the modest payments are completed, your home will receive free electricity for decades. Solar City – mentioned in this book – is a particularly large solar company which offers exceptional deals. It serves customers in 18 states. Wherever you live, make sure to get estimates from multiple solar companies to ensure that you get the best deal available.

Please always remember that if you don't own your home, you can still have a big impact by voting for solar and wind power to be implemented in your state. Critical renewable energy legislation is frequently up for voter approval and it cannot move forward without the enthusiastic support of concerned people like you and me. In fact, it is just as important to vote for and spread the word about renewables as it is to buy and invest in renewables. Coal and oil lobbies are big, powerful, and well-funded and they can skew and shade the appearance of landmark environmental legislation to make it seem like a bad idea to the average voter. Clean energy needs your assistance in the voting booth as much as anywhere. Many environmental groups and NGOs implement calling campaigns to get the word out on important legislation, and volunteering to be an earnestly concerned call operator is a giant help to them.

I should say that all renewable energy sources, including solar, wind, wave, geothermal, biomass, hydroelectric, and various biofuels, are superior alternatives to fossil fuels. They simply vary in applicability and relative environmental impact. I put such heavy emphasis on solar power and wind power because I see them as the most viable options for broad worldwide adoption with the greatest ease and least environmental impact.

EATING ORGANIC:

The best places to find organic food are at Trader Joes and Whole Foods Markets, as well as at your local farmer's market. Most mainstream supermarkets, such as Ralphs, Safeway, and Albertsons also have a small organic produce section. All organic food is labeled as organic, so make sure to check for a sticker or label.

Many organic farms are CSA – Community Supported Agriculture. These CSAs receive $20-$50 per month from hundreds of members. Members, in turn, receive a large box – usually twice a month – full of whatever fresh produce has ripened and been picked on the farm. You can usually find a CSA in your area with a quick internet search.

GIVING:

This simple idea is based on the fact that Europe, North America, Japan, Australia, and New Zealand are so wealthy compared to the developing world that giving even a small amount of money – to us – has a big and lasting impact on the poorest regions. It matters less who or what you choose to support – the environment, women, disaster relief – and more that you just offer support of some kind to the entities in the world that are truly struggling.

The following organizations turn cash donations into real, effectual, positive changes in the world. They are grouped thematically and listed in decreasing size, broadly.

The environment and animals: Greenpeace, The Nature Conservancy, World Wildlife Fund, Sierra Club, PETA, The Humane Society, The Human Farming Association, National Resources Defense Council, Friends of the Earth International, Mercy for Animals, Earth First!, Environmental Defense Fund, Amazon Watch, Rainforest Action Network, Rainforest Alliance

Human rights: Amnesty International, Human Rights Watch, The United Nations

Emergency relief/aid: OXFAM, Red Cross, World Food Programme, Salvation Army, Medicins Sans Frontieres (Doctors without Borders), Feed America

Women: CARE, UNICEF, UNIFEM, Global Fund for Women, Womankind Worldwide, Women for Women International, Pro Mujer

Developing the third world: UNESCO, UNICEF, Habitat for Humanity, Grameen Bank, Clinton Global Initiative, Kiva.org, Heifer Project International, DATA

Promotion of Peace/Conflict Resolution: The United Nations, Peace Action, Peace Corps, Anti-War Coalition, Food Not Bombs

If you are a young person or don't have money to give, as mentioned before, you can volunteer at call centers for your favorite organization and help to raise awareness or funds. Excellent opportunities to offer your physical labor or presence are available with Habitat for Humanity (www.habitat.org) which builds houses in the U.S. and in countless countries, and the Earth Corps (www.earthcorps.org) which offers a slew of pro-environment projects inside the U.S. On the local scale, community and city event calendars are filled with clean-up days, tree plantings, food drives, and recycling days that would benefit from your energy, spirit, and helping hand.

There are innumerable avenues for volunteering internationally. Two of the most broadly based groups are Service Civil International of the International Volunteer Service (www.sci-ivs.org) and Global Volunteers (www.globalvolunteers.org).

Call your local chamber of commerce, city hall, or library to inquire about volunteering in your local area. There are so many ways to give, be it donating money, making calls to raise awareness, providing physical labor for a project, or just showing up and giving your love at a home for the elderly, an orphanage, or at a talk about a topic that you believe in.

When you give, you make connections and your own abundance expands. The feeling of purpose in your life grows, and you become more than you were.

UPLIFTING WOMEN:

The easiest way to help the most disadvantaged women – those in the developing world – is to donate money to non-profit organizations such as:

www.womenforwomen.org
www.globalfundforwomen.org
www.unicef.org
www. care.org
www. womankind.org.uk
www. amnesty.org
www. promujer.org (focusing on Latin America)
www. unifem.org

Simply becoming aware of the plight of disenfranchised and oppressed women across the globe is a very powerful act in itself. Understanding archaic gender-biased beliefs in your own country and the egregious gender inequalities in repressive societies is a key to initiating change.

A good way to start is by reading *New York Times* Pulitzer Prize-winning columnist Nicholas Kristof's book, *Half the Sky: Turning Oppression into Opportunity for Women Worldwide*.

LIVING MORE EFFICIENTLY:

Recycle. If your neighborhood trash collectors do not actively recycle, virtually every city has a recycling center, as do many Ralph's supermarkets. You can bring your recyclables to these locations and get paid for the paper, plastic, aluminum, and glass that you bring. As a very young child, I can remember my neighbor, Mrs. La Fornara, enlisting us to pile newspapers to the brim of her Volkswagen van. We would bring the paper to the nearby recycling center to collect $10 to $20, which seemed like a fortune at the time.

Save energy. Buying energy-efficient home appliances is a great way to save energy all day long, every day. Another inexpensive and immediate way to save energy and CO2 is by replacing your home's light bulbs with compact fluorescent lights, or CFLs (the ones that look like a swirly-tubed ice cream cone). They use about 80% less energy than regular light bulbs and usually last seven to ten YEARS. If each American household – 110 million in all – replaced one 60-watt bulb with a CFL, the energy saved would be equivalent to turning off two entire coal-fired energy plants (1). That's just from replacing one bulb. The average

195

American home has over fifty bulb sockets. That amounts to astonishing potential energy savings from this one inexpensive, reliable, miraculous light bulb.

Using less gasoline

Buy an electric car! Most car companies currently produce all-electric zero emission cars that you can charge right at home, such as the Nissan Leaf ($30,000), the Tesla Model S and Model 3 ($35,000), as well as models by Mercedes-Benz, BMW, Fiat, Renault, Chevrolet, and the Th!nk City and Zenn Car, the latter two are available in Europe. Other companies like Reva and Mitsubishi produce electric cars for consumers in India and Asia, respectively. As part of the U.S. economic stimulus bill of 2009, thirty electric-car battery factories will soon be in operation, compared to two factories in 2008.

For the no-holds-barred "go green" enthusiast, it is possible to convert any car to an all-electric car with less trouble than you might imagine. If you are mechanically-inclined, do-it-yourself conversion kits can be purchased online, parts included, for around $5,000. For about twice that amount many private garages will do the conversion for you. To access this sizeable network of technicians and businesses, the following websites are good resources:

www.eaaev.org (Electric Automobile Association)
www.panhandleev.org
www.hybridcars.com/electric-car (the home-base for information on the subject)

Saving gasoline with a gas-powered or hybrid car is, of course, also possible. Keeping your tires properly inflated, and even buying tires that are slightly less wide are a few tricks to start with. The sudden preponderance of overly-wide "performance" tires has helped to dramatically reduce overall gas mileage of late in the United States. Even a small change in tire width will produce noticeable results. Try it!

Conserve water. By far, the most effective way to lower your personal water footprint is to eat fewer animal products. Other than that, some water-saving tips are to shorten your showers by one or two minutes (saves five gallons per day), install low-flow shower heads (saves up to 20 gallons per day), only do full loads of dishes or laundry (saves ten to fifty gallons per load of laundry), and fix leaky faucets (saves up to twenty gallons per day). These statistics are all taken from **www.bewaterwise.com**, which is a website dedicated to helping Southern California residents save water, but it is helpful to anyone who is interested in conserving water.

Also, plant vegetation in your yard that requires little, if any, irrigation, especially if you live in an arid region like the Southwestern U.S. Succulent plants, juniper bushes, shrubs, and non-broad leafed plants are good choices. Ask at your local nursery for good water-wise plant choices. If you do water your yard, do it before 8am to reduce evaporation (saves 25 gallons per day). Use a broom instead of a hose to clean driveways and sidewalks (up to 150 gallons saved each time), and check your sprinkler system for leaks, overspray, and broken sprinkler heads (up to 500 gallons per month saved).

Remember that it requires enormous amounts of energy to transport water from the natural source to residences, and it consumes large quantities of water to produce energy in traditional power plants. So saving water and energy go hand in hand!

Be globally conscious as well as health conscious about what you eat. The foods that are best for your body are also best for the planet. Eating less meat lowers your chances of acquiring multiple kinds of cancer, and it also is the number-one way to save the planet's resources.

Two things that Western denizens eat too much of are meat and sugar. Each day the average American consumes a half pound of meat and 20 teaspoons of refined sugar. We are so conditioned to these high levels of intake that some of us have come to believe that anything less would constitute an austere and incomplete diet. Quite the opposite is true. In fact, millions of people worldwide never eat sugar or meat, and rather than wasting away, they are almost invariably some of the healthiest people alive, and across myriad societies.

I do not suggest that we all become vegetarians, just that we cut down a bit on the amount and frequency of eating sugar and meat. After all, they lead to three of our biggest killers in the Western world: diabetes, atherosclerosis, and cancer. I, myself, have not eaten meat for about six years, and now I am completely vegan. I admit that being vegan takes some logistical effort at first, but that is mainly because our society and food production is geared toward meat eaters. For your body and for the planet, being vegan is much easier, and that is what's important.

Also, we should all try to eat less food from a package, can, or box because these products tend to contain preservatives, artificial colorings, artificial sweeteners, and chemical flavor enhancers. Stick to food that's fresh and in its natural form. A guideline is that if a food or product wasn't available 500 years ago, then don't eat it. Another basic guideline is to shop the perimeter of the grocery store. This is where the fresh food is kept because the chillers that keep it cool need to be plugged into wall outlets. Food in the interior of markets usually has a shelf life of six months to two years!

Citations and Bibliography

Introduction

1. Decrease in agri-chemical additives shown to decrease lung and breast cancer rates most markedly, up to 50 % over a lifetime, but commonly from 5-10%. 2-7 lbs/acre of pesticides applied at a maximum of twice weekly for the entire growth cycle of a carrot patch, sometimes including 75 lbs/acre of fumigants. Average distance organic food travels before eaten: 50 miles, average conventional food travels: 1,500 miles. 60lbs of carrots eaten/year are 0.3% of a 20,000 lb payload which generates 7220 lbs of CO_2 on 1,500 mile journey (4mpg, 19lbs of CO_2 per gallon of gas burned). U.S. taxpayers pay between $20 and $25 billion annually, depending on market conditions, for non-organic agribusiness subsidies. Asthma affects 7% of U.S. population, or 22 million people. Its main triggers are air pollution and airborne chemicals.

2. Average shower flows 3gpm (2.5gpm are low-flow, but many are 4gpm). You save 3 gallons of fresh water per day, so over 1,000 gallons of fresh water per year, which is water that was taken from fresh water habitats for fish and other wildlife in your immediate region. Also, you save 2/3 lb. of CO_2 daily by saving ½ KWh of energy by not having to heat those 3 gallons of water. This saves over 240 lb of CO_2 from going into the air annually. Based on heating standard 40 gallon water heater from 65 degrees to 140 degrees, requiring 27 million joules, which is 7.5 KWh at 3.6 million joules/KWh. 1.35lb of CO_2 produced per KWh from natural gas. 3 gallons of water is 1/13 of 40 gallons which is just over ½ KWh of energy saved or 2/3 lb. fewer of CO_2 produced.

3. Prominent NGOs such as Child Fund and Save the Children require from $24 to $32 per month to entirely sustain a child indefinitely. $50 will pay the school fees for an east African girl for a year, on average, and it will pay the fees for a Bangladeshi or Indian girl for six months, on average.

4. Averaging eight ounces (½ lb) of meat per meal, you will eat 26 fewer pounds of meat per year (one cow consumes 10,000lb of soy beans or grain in its lifetime but only yields 500 lbs. of beef. Therefore every half pound of beef that you eat, it required 10 lb. of vegetable or grain to feed and grow that beef which could have been fed to a human being). Countless studies prove the carcinogenic effects of

meat eating. One example: Michaud DS. et al. "Meat intake and bladder cancer risk in 2 prospective cohort studies." American Journal of Clinical Nutrition 2006 Nov;84(5):1177-83. 300 trees/acre of rainforest on average. Cows require two acres of grass per animal to graze and reach full weight. 600 trees to yield 500 lbs. of meat = over one tree per pound of meat consumed.

5. At 30 miles per daily commute distance national average, and one pound of CO_2 produced per mile driven in an average US car, (19.4 lbs of CO_2 produced per gallon, average US gas mileage = 20.3mpg) (http://www.epa.gov/oms/climate/420f05004.htm) you save 28 lbs of CO_2 production by not commuting one day, and you save about 7,000 lbs of CO_2 per year (240 workdays per year). $6 per day savings in gasoline by not commuting, which is $72 if done once monthly.

6. (Average U.S. home consumes, very conservatively, 20,000 KWh of energy (electricity + gas) per year. 1/3 of that from coal = 7,000 KWh, producing 14,000 lb of CO_2. 2/3 from gas = 13,000 KWh, producing 1.3 lb of CO_2 per Kwh, so about 17,000 lb of CO_2. So a total of 31,000 lb of CO_2 not going into the air if you completely convert to solar. But solar systems usually rely on grid electricity at night, when heating is still essential but lighting is only critical for a few hours, and appliance use is minimal. Therefore, 1/3 of your energy is used at night, or 10,000 lb. of CO_2. This leaves 20,000 lb. of CO_2 per year that is NOT produced/released into the air if you switch your home to solar.

7. $50 per year on average in Africa to educate a girl for a year, and $100 per year in South Asia. Every 10% that women's literacy rates rise in a given population, fertility rates drop by ½ of a child per woman, on average.

Other Sources:

Nisbett, R. 2003, *The Geography of Thought: How Asians and Westerners Think Differently...and Why.* Free Press, New York.

Geddes, R. and Lueck, D, 2002. "The Gains from Self-Ownership and the Expansion of Women's Rights." American Economic Review, American Economic Association. Vol. 92(4), pgs 1079-1092, and World Population Data Sheet 2007.

UN Development Program – Human Development Report 2006. Accessed May, 2010 from: http://www.data360.org/dsg.aspx?Data_Set_Group_Id=757

Our Beliefs Are Our Only Limitation

1. Walsch, N.D. (1995) *Conversations with God, Book 1: An Uncommon Dialogue*
2. Ray, James Arthur, 2008. *Harmonic Wealth: the secret of attracting the life you want.* Hyperion Books, New York.

Damsel in Distress

1. Steinman, Ethan (2013) "Glacial Balance" feature film
2. Steinman, Ethan (2013) and Orlowski, Jeff, (2014) "Chasing Ice" feature film
3. FAO (2015) Global Forest Resources Assessment
4. IPCC, 2007, Fourth Assessment Report: Climate Change 2007
5. Church, J. and N. White (2006) "A 20th-century acceleration in global sea level rise," *Geophysical Research Letters* 33(1).
6. Rahmstorf, S (2007) "A Semi-empirical Approach to Predicting Future Sea-Level Rise," *Science* 315(5810).
7. Clark, Robert P. 2000, *Global Life Systems: Population, food, and disease in the process of globalization.* Rowman & Littlefield, Oxford UK, pg 282, and Gore, A. 2005, documentary film "An Inconvenient Truth."
8. Antholis W. and Talbott S., 2010 "Leaving a Good Legacy: Why the ethical case for combating climate change is one that should appeal to conservatives." *Time magazine*, June 14, pg 24.
9. Oster S. 2006, "Illegal Power Plants, Coal Mines in China Pose Challenge for Beijing." *The Wall Street Journal*, Dec. 27.
10. Goodland, R. and J. Anhang (2009) "Livestock and climate change: what if the key actors in climate change are... cows, pigs, and chickens?"
11. Kunzig, Robert, "World Without Ice" National Geographic, October 2011
12. Wald M., 2007, "Science Panel Disputes Estimates of US Coal Supply." *New York Times*, June 21.
13. www.guardian.co.uk/environment/datablog/2009dec/07/copenhagen-climate-change-summit, Accessed May 2010.
14. www.wikipedia.org/globalco2emissions, Accessed April 2010.
15. http://sd.defra.gov.uk/2010/03/fighting-the-scourge-of-illegal-logging-sustainable- developtment-in-action/, Accessed May 2010.
16. www.ran.org/palm_oil (accessed May 13, 2016)
17. www.rainforests.mongabay.com/1024.htm, Accessed May 2010.
18. Antholis W. and Talbott S., 2010. "Leaving a Good Legacy: Why the ethical case for combating climate change is one that should appeal to conservatives." *Time Magazine,* June 14, pg. 24.

Other Sources:

Hansen, Matthew C., et al. (2013) "High-resolution global maps of 21st-century forest cover change." *Science* 342.6160: 850-853.

The Source of Our Problems

1.Harvey, D. 2011. "The Party of Wall Street Meets its Nemesis" Verso Books blog, Aug. 28. http://www.versobooks.com/blogs/777-david-harvey-the-party-of-wall-street-meets-its-nemesis (accessed Dec.11, 2012).
2. http://www.heritage.org/research/reports/2007/06/how-farm-subsidies-harm-taxpayers-   consumers-and-farmers-too (Accessed July 2011).
3. Symington, A. 2005 "From Tragedy and Injustice to Rights and Empowerment: accountability in the economic realm" within Wilson, Shamillah, Anasuya Sengupta, and Kristy Evans, Eds., 2005. *Defending Our Dreams: Global feminist voices for a new generation.* Zed Books, London, pg. 40.
4. Offen, K. 2004. "Historical Political Ecology: An Introduction." *Historical Geography* 32: 19-42.
5. Postman, Niel, 1985. *Amusing Ourselves to Death*, Penguin Books, New York.

The Source of Our Solutions

1. United Nations Publications, 2006. "In-Depth Study on All Forms of Violence against Women" Report of the Secretary General. A/61/122/Add.1. 6 July.
2. *World Bank Study World Development Report,* 1993 "Investing in Health", New York, Oxford University Press.

Why is Our Population Exploding?

1. Concept taken from Gore, A. 2005, "An Inconvenient Truth" documentary film.
2. www.worldatlas.com, Accessed February 2010.
3. www.overpopulation.org, Accessed February 2010.
4. World Population Data Sheet 2009 and www.oxfam.com
5. Boserup, E. (1965) *The Conditions of Agricultural Growth*, Aldine.
6. McGovern, G. 2001. "The Real Cost of Hunger," Accessed June 2010 from http://www.thefreelibrary.com/The+real+cost+of+hunger-a086062268

7. Frank, Andre Gunder, 1967, *Capitalism and Underdevelopment in Latin America: historical studies of Chile and Brazil.* Monthly Review Press Classics, New York.

Other Sources:

Christopherson, R., 2010. *Elemental Ecosystems*, Pearson Prentice-Hall, New Jersey, pg. 542.

Kiesel, L. 2009. "Why is the Media Afraid to Tackle Livestock's Role in Climate Change?" November 3, www.solveclimate.com, Accessed in February 2010.

UN Food and Agriculture Organization Report, 2008.

The Other Side of America's Wars

1. http://www.politicususa.com/en/cut-defense
2. http://en.wikipedia.org/wiki/National_debt_by_U.S._presidential_terms
3. Thompson, Mark, "How to Save a Trillion Dollars," Time Magazine. April 14, 2011.
4. Thompson, Mark, 2011.
5. Thompson, Mark, 2011
6. http://www.nytimes.com/2010/06/14/world/asia/14minerals.html. Accessed September 2011.
7. Harman, Danna, 2005. Christian Science Monitor, August 16, "Mexicans take over drug trade to U.S: With Colombian cartels in shambles, Mexican drug lords run the show."
8. Bulmer-Thomas, Victor, and James Dunkerley, Eds., 1999. *The United States and Latin America: The New Agenda.* Institute of Latin American Studies at University of London.
9. Gerber, Jurg, and Eric L. Jensen, Ed., 2001. *Drug War American Style.* Garland. New York.
10. Amnesty International 1990: 70.
11. Huggins, M.K. 1991. "Vigilantism and the State in Modern Latin America," in M.K. Huggins Ed., *U.S. Supported State Terror – A History of Police Training in Latin America* (pp. 219-242) Praeger. New York.
12. Gerber, 2001: 182
13. www.whitehousedrugpolicy.gov, Accessed September 2006.

14. Schweich, Thomas, 2008. New York Times "Is Afghanistan a Narco-state?" July 27.
15. Schweich, Thomas, 2008.
16. Schweich, Thomas, 2008.
17. Astorga, Luis, UNESCO discussion paper no. 36, "Drug Trafficking in Mexico: A first General Assessment."
18. Rashid, Ahmed, 2008. *Descent into Chaos: The United States, and the Failure of Nation Building in Pakistan, Afghanistan, and Central Asia.* Penguin Books, New York.
19. Dreyfuss, Robert, 2005. *Devil's Game: How the United States Helped Unleash Fundamentalist Islam.* New York, NY. Metropolitan Books, pg. 326.
20. Schweich, Thomas, 2008.

Other Sources:

Allen, Christian M. 2005. *An Industrial Geography of Cocaine.* Routledge.

Bagley, Bruce M., and William O. Walker III, Eds., 1994. *Drug trafficking in the Americas. Transaction Publishers.*

Joyce, Elizabeth and Carlos Melanuel, Eds. 1988. *Latin America and the Multi-national Drug Trade.* MacMillan Press.

Mabry, Donald J. Ed., 1989. *The Latin American Narcotics Trade and US National Security.* Greenwood Press. Westport, CT.

MacDonald, Scott B. 1988. *Dancing on a Volcano.* Praeger.

Morales, Edmundo, 1989. *Cocaine: White Gold Rush in Peru.* University of Arizona Press.

Murillo, Mario A. 2004. *Colombia and the United States: War, Unrest, and Destabilization.* Seven Stories Press. New York.

Vellinga, Menno, Ed., 2004. *The Political Economy of the Drug Industry: Latin America and the International System.* University Press of Florida, Gainsville.

Zirnite, P. 1998. "The Militarization of the Drug War in Latin America." *Current History* 97: 166-173.

Returning to Organic Agriculture

1. Garcia, Deborah Koons, 2001. "The Future of Food." Motion Picture.
2. Duram, Leslie A., 2005.*Good Growing: Why Organic Farming Works.* University of Nebraska Press, Lincoln and London.
3.Worthington, V. (1998) "Effect of Agricultural Methods on Nutritional Quality: A comparison organic with conventional crops," *Alternative Therapies* 4(1): 58-69
4. Worthington, V. (2001) "Nutritional Quality of Organic Versus Conventional Fruits, Vegetables, and Grains." *Journal of Alternative and Complimentary Medicine.* 7(2): 161-173
5. Byrum, A. "Organically Grown Foods Higher in Cancer-Fighting Chemicals than Conventionally Grown Foods." American Cancer Society Public Release. Accessed March 2003 from http://www.eurekaalert.org/pub_pubreleases/2003-03/acs-ogfo30303.php.
6. Duram, 2005: 5.
7.Worthington, V. (1998)
8. Worthington, V. (2001)
9. Byrum, (2003)
10. Byrum, (2003)
11. Kuepper, George, and Lange Cegner, 2004. *Organic Crop Production Overview.* National Sustainable Agriculture Information Service. August.
12. Kuepper and Cegner, 2004.
13. Berry, Wendell, 1977. *The Unsettling of America: Culture and Agriculture.* San Francisco. Sierra Club Books. From Duram, Leslie A., 2005.
14. *Eco-Farming: The Chinese Experience.* 2000. Published through the United Nations Environment Program (UNEP).
15. USDA, National Agricultural Statistics Service (2015) "June Agricultural Survey" accessed at http://www.ers.usda.gov/data-products/adoption-of-genetically-engineered-crops-in-the-us/recent-trends-in-ge-adoption.aspx on March 25, 2016
16. Duram, 2005.
17. Jaffe, Gregory A., 2001. *Lessen the Fear of Genetically Engineered Crops.* Christian Science Monitor, August 8, pg. 8.
18. Magdoff, Foster, and Buttel, 2000.
19. Taken from documentary motion picture "Food, Inc."
20. Tewolde, B., 2001, "The Use of Genetically Modified Crops in Agriculture and Food Production and Their Impacts on the Environment – a Developing World Perspective." Ethiopia: Ethiopian Environmental Protection Authority, p. 1.

21. Peter, D. and Ghesquiere, P. Bilan, 1988. *des connaissances et des applications de l'agriculture biologique et interet pour l'agriculture Communautaire.* Commission of the European Communities, Brussels.
22. Lampkin, N.H. and S. Padel, Eds., 1994. *The Economics of Organic Farming: An International Perspective.* Cab International, Wallingford.

Other Sources:

Curl, Cynthia L. Richard A Fenske, and Kai Elgethun 2003. "Organi-phosphorous Pesticide Exposure of Urban and Suburban Preschool Children with Organic and Conventional Diets." *Environmental Health Perspectives* 111 (3): 377-382

Dimitri, Carolyn and Catherine Green. 2002. "Recent Growth Patterns in the US Organic Foods Market." *USDA Economic Research Service, Agriculture Information Bulletin no. 777.*

Faeth, P., R. Repetto, K. Kroll, Q. Dai, and G. Helmers, 1991. *Paying the Farm Bill: U.S. Agricultural Policy and the Transition to Sustainable Agriculture.* World Resources Institute, Washington, D.C.

Green, Catherine, and Amy Kremen. 2003. "US Organic Farming in 2000-2002: Adoption of Certified Systems." *USDA Economic Research Service, Agriculture Information Bulletin no. 780.*

Heaton, Shane, 2001. "Organic Farming, Food Quality, and Human Health Report. Briefing Sheet." UK Soil Association. http://www.soilassociation.org/web/sa/saweb.nsf.librarytitoles/briefing_shee ts03- 8200a, Accessed November 2005.

OECD Working Papers, 2000. "Comparing the Profitability of Organic and Conventional Farming: The Impact of Support on Arable Farming in France."

"Organic Agriculture and Rural Poverty Alleviation." 2002. Economic and Social Commission for Asia and the Pacific Potential and Best Practices in Asia. United Nations. New York.

"Organic Food and Beverages: World Supply and Major European Markets." 1999. International Trade Centre, Geneva.

Pedersen, Lisbeth, S. Rasmussen, S. Bugel, L. Jargensen, L. Dragsted, V. Gundersen, and B. Sandstrom, 2003. "Effects of Diets Based on Foods from Conventional Versus Organic Production and Intake and Excretion of Flavinoids and Markers of Defence in Humans." *Journal of Agricultural and Good Chemistry.* 51 (19): 5671-76.

Pesticide Action Network of North America, 2003.

Swanby, H. and Wilson, S., 2005. "Smoke screen or solution? Genetic engineering and food insecurity," within Wilson, Shamillah, Anasuya Sengupta, and Kristy Evans, Eds. *Defending Our Dreams: Global feminist voices for a new generation.* Zed Books, London.

Wilson, Shamillah, Anasuya Sengupta, and Kristy Evans, Eds., 2005. *Defending Our Dreams: Global feminist voices for a new generation.* Zed Books, London.

"World Markets for Organic Fruit and Vegetables: Opportunities for developing countries in the production and export of organic horticultural products." 2001. International Trade Centre, Technical Centre for the Agricultural and Rural Cooperation. Food and Agriculture Organization of the United Nations. Rome.

Worldwatch Paper 73. 1986. "Beyond the Green Revolution: New approaches for Third World Agriculture." October.

http://www.wikipedia.org/wiki/organoponicos, Accessed February 2007.

The Miracle of Solar Power

1. *http://www.cnbc.com/id/17483073/Ted_Turner_Touts_Solar_Power_And_Invests_In_It*, Accessed November, 2009.
2. www.eia.gov/cneaf/electricity/page/co2_report/co2report/html#electric, Accessed June 2011.
3. www.eia.gov/cneaf/electricity/page/co2_report/co2report/html#electric, Accessed June 2011.
4. U.S. Energy Information Administration: http://www.eia.doe.gov/oiaf/ieo/highlights.html, Accessed July 2010.

5. Butler, Declan, 2007."Solar Power: California's latest gold rush." Nature, 450 (6).

6. Kryza, Frank, 2003. *The Power of Light: The Epic Story of Man's Quest to Harness the Sun.* McGraw-Hill, XIII.

7. Kryza, Frank, 2003.

8. Kryza, Frank, 2003.

9. Carless, Jennifer, 1993. *Renewable Energy: a Concise Guide to Green Alternatives.* Walker and Company, New York.

10. "Solar Power to the Masses," Institute of Science in Society Report July 31, 2008.

11. Pyper, J. (2015) "The Global Solar PV Market Hit 177GW in 2014, A Tenfold Increase From2008" www.greentechmedia.com

12. Shahan, Z. (2015) "Global Solar Power Capacity About To Hit 200 GW" www.cleantechnica.com

13. Kasperkevic, J (2012) "US solar industry now employs more workers than oil and gas, says report," *The Guardian*, January 12

14. http://www.businessgreen.com/business-green/news/2259302/sunedison-eyeing-plans-world, Accessed June 2010.

15. Bradford, Travis, 2006. *Solar Revolution: the Economic Transformation of the Global Energy Industry.* MIT Press.

16. Bradford, 2006.

17. Freeman, David S. 2007. *Wining Our Energy Independence: An energy insider shows how.* Gibbs Smith, Salt Lake City.

18. http://www.msnbc.msn.com/id/16577883/, Accessed May 2010.

19. IEA (2015) "Key World Energy Statistics" report

20. Smitha, E. (2012) *Screwing Mother Nature for Profit*

21. Wilson, E.O. (2012) *On Human Nature*, and MacArthur and Wilson (2015) *TheoryOf Island Biogeography*

22.http://www.cnbc.com/id/17483073/Ted_Turner_Touts_Solar_Power_And_Invests_In_It, Accessed May 2010.

23. Bradford, 2006.

Other Sources:

Beattie, Donald A. Ed., 1997. *History and Overview of the Solar Heat Technologies.* MIT Press Cambridge and London.

Fanchi, John R., 2005. *Energy in the 21st Century.* World Scientific Publishing.

Halacy, D.S. Jr., 1973. *The Coming Age of Solar Energy*. Harper and Row Publishers. New York.

Knight, Matthew, 2010. "A Dazzling Future for Solar Power?" May 12, CNN.com

Miyake, Jun, Yasuo Igarashi, and Matthias Rogner, Eds., 2004. *Biohydrogen III, Renewable Energy Systems by Biological Solar Energy Converstion*. Elsevier. Oxford.

Renewables Information: 2006. International Energy Agency. OECD/IEA.

Stanley, Tom, 2004. *Going Solar: Understanding and Using the Warmth in Sunlight*. Stonefield Pubulishing.

http://apps1.eere.energy.gov/news/news_detail.cfm/news_id=11490, Accessed June 2010.

Trafficking in Sex

1. Campagna, Daniel S., and Donald L. Poffenberger, 1988. *The Sexual Trafficking in Children: An Investigation of the Child Sex Trade*. Auburn House, Dover, Mass.
2. UN estimates, found in State Department Trafficking in Persons Report, 2003.
3. ILO, A global alliance against forced labor: 2005.
4. http://www.pbs.org/wgbh/pages/frontline/slaves/etc/stats.html, Accessed March 2006.
5. http://www.unescobkk.org/index.php?id=1022, Accessed March 2006.
6. U.S. Department of State. 2004. *Trafficking in Persons Report*. Washington, D.C.: U.S. Department of State.
7. http://www.nationmaster.com/graph/cri_rap_percap-crime-rapes-per-capita. Accessed Sept. 2011.
8. Schwartz, G.J.1999. "Empowerment and Denigration: the ambivalence of femininity in modern Thai society." Paper completed and presented in Hartshorne seminar, University of Wisconsin, Madison Geography department.
9. Marx, K (1996)[1867], Capital: A Critique of Political Economy. National Book Network
10. Sauer, C. O. (1938). Theme of plant and animal destruction in economic history. *Journal of Farm Economics*, *20*(4), 765-775.

11. Isla, A. (2006). Teoría social. La tragedia de los enclaustramientos: una perspectiva eco-feminista de la venta de oxígeno y la prostitución en Costa Rica. *Revista de ciencias sociales*, (111), 57-69.

12. Jackson, C. (1993) Women/nature or gender/history? A critique of ecofeminist 'development.' Journal of Peasant Studies, 20(3): 389-419

13. Shiva, V. (1989) *Staying Alive: women, ecology and development*, Zed Books, London.

14. Clawson, David L. and Merrill L. Johnson, 2003. *World Regional Geography: A development approach.* Prentice Hall, 510.

15. "Owed Justice: Thai Women Trafficked into Debt Bondage in Japan," 2000. Human Rights Watch. New York, Washington. Pgs. 25-26.

16. "Owed Justice," 2000.

17. ILO, A global alliance against forced labor: 2005.

18. Troubnikoff, Anna M. Ed., 2003. *Trafficking in Women and Children: Current Issues and   Developments,* Nova Publishing, New York.

19. Troubnikoff, 2003.

20. "Owed Justice: Thai Women Trafficked into Debt Bondage in Japan," 2000: 6.

21. Skrobanek, Siriphon, Nattaya Bookpakdi, and Chutima Janthakeero, 1997. *The traffic in women: human realities of the international sex trade.* Zed Books. London.

22. Asia Migrant Bulletin. July-December, 1995. Volume III. No. 3&4.

23. UN estimates, found in State Department Trafficking in Persons Report, 2003.

24. Williams, Phil, Ed., 1999. *Illegal Immigration and Commercial Sex: The New Slave Trade.* Frank Cass. London.

25. Williams, 1999.

26. Hawkins, D. 2002, *Power vs. Force: The Hidden Determinants of Human Behavior*. Hay House, Carlsbad, California, p. 216.

27. Schwartz, G.J.1999.

28. Skrobanek, S., Bookpakdi, N., and Janthakeero, C., 1997.

29. Transcribed interview from television show "Rediscovering Biology: Molecular to Global Perspectives," on Oregon Public Broadcasting, 30 April 2010.

30. UNICEF Progress for Children Report, 2007.

31. Chrisler, J. within Within Paludi, Michele A. Ed. *Feminism and Women's Rights Worldwide*, Vol. 3. ABC CLIO Press, Santa Barbara.

32. Clawson and Johnson, 2003.

Other Sources:

Austin, J.L., J.O. Urmson and Marina Sbisa, eds., 1975. *How to Do Things with Words*. Cambridge, MA: Harvard University Press.

Bell, David et. al. Eds., 2001. *Pleasure Zones: Bodies, Cities, Spaces.* Syracuse University Press.

Brennan, Denise, 2004. *What's Love Got to Do with it: Transnational Desires and Sex Tourism in the Dominican Republic*. Durham, NC: Duke University Press.

Butler, Judith. 1997. The *Psychic Life of Power: Theories in Subjection*. Stanford University Press.

Foucault, Michel, 1990. *The History of Sexuality, Vol I-III*. Vintage Books, New York.

Hubbard, Phil, 1998, "Sexuality, Immorality and the City: Red-Light Districts and the Marginalization of Female Street Prostitutes." *Gender, Place & Culture: A Journal of Feminist Geography,* 5(1): 55-76.

Ingold, Tim, 1993. "Globes and Spheres: The topology of environmentalism." In Kay Milton, ed. *Environmentalism.* New York: Routledge. 31-42.

Jeffrey, Leslie Ann, 2002. *Sex and Borders: Gender, National Identity, and Prostitution Policy in Thailand.* UBC Press. Vancuver.

Kempadoo, Kamala, and Doezema Jo. Eds., 1998. *Global Sex Workers: Rights, Resistance, and Redefinition.* Routledge, New York.

Laqueur, Thomas Walter, 1992. *Making Sex: Body and Gender from the Greeks to Freud.* Harvard University Press.

Martin, E., 1994. *Flexible Bodies: tracking immunity in American culture from the Days of Polio to the Age of AIDS*. Beacon Press.

Pattanaik, Bandana, and Susanne Thorbek, Eds., 2002. *Transnational Prostitution: changing global patterns.* Zed Books. London, 123.

Seabrook, Jeremy. 2001. *Travels in the Skin Trade: Tourism and the Sex Industry.* Pluto Press. London.

Steady, Filomina Chioma, 2002. *Black Women, Globalization, and Economic Justice: Studies from Africa and the African Diaspora.* Schenkman Books. Rochester, Vermont.

UNESCO 2009, The State of the World's Children Report and ILO, A global alliance against forced labor: 2005.

Visweswaran, Kamala, 1994. Fictions of Feminist Ethnography. University of Minnesota Press.

White, Luise, 1994. The *Comforts of Home: Prostitution in Colonial Nairobi.* University of Chicago Press.

http://www.usinfo.state.gov/gi/Archive/2004/May/12-381449.html, Accessed April 2010.

Addicted to Dirty Fuels, By Design

1. Singh, Madanjeet, 1998. *The Timeless Energy of the Sun for Life and Peace with Nature.* Unesco Publishing.
2. http://en.wikipedia.org/wiki/World_energy_resources_and_consumption, Accessed July 2010.
3. http://www.itopf.com/information-services/data-and-statistics/statistics/, accessed Sept. 2011.
4. Leech, Garry., 2006. *Crude Interventions: The United States, Oil, and the New Global (Dis)Order.* Zed Books. London and New York, 29.
5. Vidal, Gore, 2003. *Dreaming War: Blood for Oil and the Cheney/Bush Junta.* Nation Books. New York, 13.
6. Leech, 2006: 36.
7. Leech, 2006: 32.
8. "Alaska's Last Oil," National Georaphic Channel, November 2009.
9. "Alaska's Last Oil," National Georaphic Channel, November 2009.
10. U.S. Minerals Management Service Statistics, 2011.
11. http://www.itopf.com/information-services/data-and-statistics/statistics/#no, Accessed May 2006.
12. "Could shale gas power the world?" Walsh, Bryan. Time Magazine, April 11, 2011.

13. Gelbspan, Ross., 2004. *Boiling Point: How Politicians, Big Oil and Coal, Journalists, and Activists are Fueling the Climate Crisis – and What we can do to Avert Disaster.* Basic Books. New York.

14. Bykoff, Maxwell T. and Jules M., 2004. "Balance as Bias: Global Warming and the U.S. Prestige Press." *Global Environmental Change* (14), 125-136.

15. Harper's Index 2003.

16. Gelbspan, 2004: 51.

17. "Could shale gas power the world?" Walsh, Bryan. Time Magazine, April 11, 2011.

18. http://en.wikipedia.org/wiki/Coal_mining, accessed Sept. 2011.

19. National Geographic Magazine, March 2011.

20. "Could shale gas power the world?" Walsh, 2011.

21. Bradford, T. and Katzman, M., 2006. *Solar and Wind Energy: An Economic Evaluation of Current and Future Technologies.* Rowman and Littlefield.

22. Carless, Jennifer, 1993. *Renewable Energy: a Concise Guide to Green Alternatives.* Walker and Company, New York.

Other Sources:

Everest, Larry, 2004. *Oil Power, and Empire: Iraq and the US Global Agenda.* Common Courage Press.

Klare, Michael T., 2001. *Resource Wars: the New Landscape of Global Conflict.* Henry Holt and Company. New York.

Klare, Michael T., 2004. *Blood and Oil: the dangers and consequences of America's Growing Dependency.* Henry Hold and Company, 59.

Miller, David Ed., 2004. *Tell Me Lies: propaganda and media distortion in the attack on Iraq. Pluto Press.*

Miniter, Richard, 2004. *Shadow War: the Untold Story of How Bush is Winning the War on Terror.* Regenery Publishing, Inc. Washington, D.C.

Pelletiere, Stephen, 2004. *America's Oil Wars.* Praeger.

Pilger, John, 2002. *The New Rulers of the World.* Verso, London and New York.

Scott, Peter Dale, 2003. *Drugs, Oil, and War.* Rowan & Littlefield.

Sperry, Paul, 2003. *Crude Politics.* WND Books.

Yetiv, Steve A., 2004. *Crude Awakenings: Global Oil Security and American Foreign Policy.* Cornell University Press.

http://www.telegraph.co.uk/news/worldnews/asia/afghanistan/8085296/Hamid-Karzai-admits-office-receives-bags-of-money-from-Iran.html, accessed Sept. 6, 2011.

http://envirowonk.com/content/view/68/1/,, accessed Sept. 15, 2011.

The Rise of Women

1. Momsen, Janet Henshall, 1991. *Women and Development in the Third World.* Routledge, London.
2. As quoted from appearance on "The Oprah Winfrey Show", April 13, 2010.
3. Momsen, 1991.
4. Momsen, 1991.
5. http://www.ipu.org/wmn-e/suffrage.htm (accessed July 5, 2016)
6. http://www.globalfundforwomen.org accessed June 2010.
7. *World Bank Study World Development Report,* 1993 "Investing in Health", New York, Oxford University Press.
8. Momsen, 1991.
9. FAO, 2002 "Gender and Food Security," accessed from http://www.fao.org/gender/en/agri-e.htm>.
10. Kristof, Nicholas D. "Sewing Her Way Out of Poverty." September 14, 2011. New York Times The Opinion Pages.
11. Paludi M., Martin J., Paludi C., Boggess S., Hicks K., Speech L., 2010. "Pay Equity as justice: United States and International Perspectives." Within Paludi, Michele A. Ed. *Feminism and Women's Rights Worldwide*, Vol. 3. ABC CLIO Press, Santa Barbara.
12. U.S. Bureau of Labor Statistics (2013) "Highlights of Women's Earnings in 2013"Report 1051
13. Momsen, 1991.
14. Momsen, 1991.
15. United Nations Population Fund Activities Report, 2005.
16. UNICEF Progress for Children Report, 2007.
17. UNICEF Progress for Children Report, 2007.

18. Charles M. and Bradley K. 2002, "Equal but Separate: A cross-national study of sex segregation in higher education." *American Sociological Review*, 67, 573-599.

19. UN Population Fund Activities Report, 2005.

20. Sharma, Om Parkash and Robert D. Tetherford, 1990. *Effect of Female Literacy on Fertility in India.* New Delhi: Office of the Registrar General & Census Commissioner, and Ministry of Home Affairs, Government of India, pg. 27.

21. Basow, Susan, "Women in Education: Students and Professors Worldwide" within Paludi, Michele A. Ed. 2010. Vol 1.

22. Basow within Paludi, 2010, vol. 1.

23. Sharma and Tetherford, 1990.

24. Sharma and Tetherford, 1990.

25. Brizendine, L. 2006. "The Female Brain," Broadway Books, New York.

26. Eagley, A.H. and Hohanneson-Schmidt, M.C. 2001, "The Leadership Styles of Women and Men." *Journal of Social Issues*, 57, 781-797 and Walumba, Wi, and Ojode, 2004, "Gender and Instructional Outcomes: The mediating role of leadership style." *Journal of Management Development*, 23, 124-140, Within Haddad, et. al. 2010.

27. Eagly and Hohanneson-Schmidt, 2001, and Walumba and Ojode, 2004.

28. Haddad within Paludi, Michele A, 2010. Vol.1, pg. 98.

29. Sen, Gita, Adrienne Germain, and Lincoln C. Chen, 1994, pg. 71.

30. Hamad, Tajeldin, Frederick Swarts, and Anne Ranniste Smart, Eds., 2003. *Culture of Responsibility and the Role of NGOs.* Continuum International Publishing Group.

31. Blumberg, Rae Lesser, et al. Eds., 1995. *EnGENDERing Wealth and Well-Being: Empowerment for Global Change.* Westview Press, Boulder.

32. Blumberg, 1995.

33. UNICEF: Progress for Children Report, 2007.

34. UNICEF: Progress for Children Report, 2007.

35. Diop-Sidibe, Campbell, & Becker, 2005, "Domestic Violence Against Women in Egypt: Wife beating and health outcomes." Social Science & Medicine, 62, 1260-1277 and Chrisler, Joan and Cynthia Garrett, "Women's Reproductive Rights: An International Perspective." Within Paludi, 2010, vol. 3.

36. Pettifor, Measham, Reef, & Padian, 2004, "Sexual Power and HIV Risk, South Africa. Emerging Infectious Diseases." Accessed May 2010 from http://www.cdc.gov/ncidod/EID/vol10no11/04-0252.htm.

37. UNICEF: Progress for Children, 2005.

38. Steinem, Gloria, 2010. "A child bride, fighting for her rights," *Time* magazine, May 10, pg. 148.

39. Ahmed, Aziza, 2005. "Chanelling Discourse, Effecting Change: young women and sexual rights." Within Wilson, Shamillah, Anasuya Sengupta, and Kristy Evans, Eds. *Defending Our Dreams: Global feminist voices for a new generation.* Zed Books, London.

40. Butt, R. 2009, "Condom use could make HIV/AIDS situation worse in Africa, says Pope: controversy over Catholic church's stance reignited – Policy divides some clergy working with patients." *Guardian,* p. 18.

41. UNICEF: Progress for Children, 2007.

42. UNICEF, 2007 pg. 30 and UNICEF 2009, The State of the World's Children Report, Table 4: HIV/AIDS and Table 8: Women.

43. Garcia-Moreno, C. Jansen, H.A.F.M., Ellseberg, M., Heise, L.L. and Watts, C.H. 2005, WHO multi-country study on women's health and domestic violence against women: initial results on prevalence, health outcomes and women's responses. Switzerland: World health Organization.

44. Stiglmayer, A. 1993, "A pattern of rape: A torrent of wrenching first-person testimonies tells of a now Serb atrocity: Systematic sexual abuse." *Newsweek.* Accessed May2010 at http://www.newsweek.com/id/115892.

45. Swiss, S. & Giller, J. 1993, "Rape as a crime of war: A medical perspective." *Journal of the American Medical Association,* 270, 612-615.

46. Amnesty International, 2004. "Lives blown apart: crimes against women in armed conflict." London: Amnesty International Publications. Accessed May 2010 from http://www.amnesty.org/en/library/info/ACT77/075/2004.

47. Sen, 1994, pg. 143.

48. Blumberg, 1995, pg. 155.

Other Sources:

Domosh, Mona and Joni Seager, 2001. *Putting Women in Place.* New York: Guilford Press.

Dreze, J.P., and A.K. Sen, 1989. *Hunger and Public Action.* Oxford: Clarendon Press.

Duran, Lydia A., Noel D. Payne, and Anahi Russo, Eds., 2007. *Building Feminist Movements and Organizations: Global Perspectives.* Zed Books, London.

Eagley and Carli, 2007. *Through the Labyrinth.* Boston: Harvard Business School Press.

Elias, Marlene and Judith Carney., 2005. "Shea Butter, Globalization, and the Women of Burkina Faso." In Lise Nelson and Joni Seager, eds., *A Companion to Feminist Geography*. Malden, MA: Blackwell Publishing. 93-108.

Erler, Mary C. and Maryanne Kowaleski, Eds., 2003. *Gendering the Master Narrative: Women and Power in the Middle Ages*, Cornell University Press, Ithaca.

Fraser, Arvonne S., and Irene Tinker, Eds., 2004. Developing Power: How Women Transformed International Development. The Feminist Press at The City University of New York. New York.

Haddad E., and Schweinle W. "The Feminine Political Persona: Queen Victoria, Ellen Johnson Sirleaf, and Michelle Bachelet." Within Paludi, 2010, vol. 1.

Haraway, Donna, 1991. *Simians, Cyborgs, and Women*. London: Free Association Books. 127-148.

Harding, Sandra, ed., 2004. *The Feminist Standpoint Theory Reader*. New York: Routledge.

Hooks, Bell, 2000. *Feminism is for Everybody: Passionate Politics*. Cambridge, MA: Southend Press.

Massey, Doreen, 1994. *Space, Place and Gender,* Minneapolis: University of Minnesota.

McGuire , Judy, and Barry Popkin, 1990. "Helping Women Improve Nutrition in the Developing World: Beating the Zero-Sum Game," World Bank technical Paper, no. 114 (Washington, DC: WorldBank.

Medrano, Diana, and Rodrigo Villar, 1988. *Mujer campasina y organizacion rural en Colombia: Tres estudios de caso*, Press of Universidad de los Andes (CEREC).

Mithers, C. 2004, "The garden of evil." Accessed May 2010 from http://www.globalfundforwomen.org/cms/press-center/2004-gfw-news/garden-of-evil.html

Paludi, Michele A. Ed., 2010. *Feminism and Women's Rights Worldwide Vol. 1,2,3.* ABC CLIO Press, Santa Barbara.

Parpart, Jane L., Shirin M. Rai, and Kathleen Staudt, Eds., 2002. *Rethinking Empowerment: Gender and development in a global/local world.* Routledge, London.

Sangari, Kumkum, and Uma Chakravarti, Eds., 1999. *From Myths to Markets: Essays on Gender.* Manohar Publishers, New Delhi.

Sen, Gita, Adrienne Germain, and Lincoln C. Chen, 1994. *Population Policies Reconsidered: Health, Empowerment, and Rights.* Harvard University Press.

Viswanath, Vanita, 1991. *NGOs and Women's Develoment in Rural South India: A Comparative Analysis.* Westview Press, Boulder.

Wilson, Shamillah, Anasuya Sengupta, and Kristy Evans, Eds., 2005. *Defending Our Dreams: Global feminist voices for a new generation.* Zed Books, London.

"More Catholic bishops deny communion to pro-choice politicians." October 2004, *Church & State*, p. 19-20.

The Power of Giving

1. *Time* Magazine, May 10, 2010. "The 100 Most Influential People in the World."
2. Gaudiani, Claire, 2003. *The Greater Good: How Philanthropy Drives the American Economy and Can Save Capitalism.* Times Books.
3. Fleishman, Joel L. 2007. "Philanthropic Leadership: A Personal Perspective." Presentation to HSBC Bank, USA. Accessed May 2007 from http://us.hsbc.com/privatebanking/wealth/pb_fleishman.asp.
4. www.givingusa.org/giving-usa-2015-press-release (accessed May 13, 2016)
5. Gaudiani, 2003.
6. *Time* Magazine, May 10, 2010. "The 100 Most Influential People in the World."
7. Smith, J. (2013) "America's Most Generous Companies" Forbes online, July 16
8. Union of International Associations, 2004.
9. Auletta, Ken, 2004. *Media Man: Ted Turner's Improbable Empire.* Atlas Books, 30.
10. Auletta, 2004.

11. http://www.turnerfoundation.org, Accessed November 2006.
12.http://www.renewableenergyworld.com/rea/news/article/2010/03/southern-company-ted-turner-acquire-first-solar-project, Accessed July 2010.
13. Gaudiani, 2003: 17
14. http://www.oprah.com, Accessed December 2006.
15. http://www.learningtogive.org, Accessed January 2007.

Other Sources:

Adam, Thomas, Ed., 2004. *Philanthropy, Patronage, and Civil Society: Experiences from Germany, Great Britain, and North America.* Indiana University Press.

Bonner, Michael, Mine Ener, Amy Singer, Eds., 2003. *Poverty and Charity in Middle Eastern Contexts.* State University of New York Press.

Bryant, Raymond L., 2005. *Nongovernmental Organizations in Environmental Struggles: Politics and the Making of Moral Capital in the Philippines.* Yale University Press

Clift, Elayne, Ed., 2005. *Women, Philanthropy, and Social Change: Vision for a just society.* Tufts University Press.

De Borms, Luc Tayart, 2005. *Foundations: Creating Impact in a Globalised World.* John Wiley & Sons, Ltd.

Eversole, Robyn Ed., 2003 *Here to Help: NGOs Combating Poverty in Latin America.* M.E. Sharpe. New York and London.

Gasman, Marybeth and Katherine V. Sedgwick Eds., 2005. *Uplifting a People.* Peter Lang.

Gregory, Robert G., 1992. *The Ride and Fall of Philanthropy in East Africa: The Asian Contribution.* Transaction Publishers.

Gunter, Michael M. Jr. *Building the Next Ark: How NGOs Work to Protect Biodiversity.* Dartmouth College Press, 2004.

Hamad, Tajeldin, Frederick Swarts, and Anne Ranniste Smart, Eds., 2003. *Culture of Responsibility and the Role of NGOs.* Continuum International Publishing Group.

Ieere, Wybo P. Ed., 2004. *From Government to Governance: The Growing Impact of Non-state Actors in the International and European Legal System.* TMC Asser Press. The Hague.

Ielmut Anheier and Diana Leat, Eds., 2006. *Creative Philanthropy: toward a new philanthropy for the 21st century.* Routledge Press.

Iopgood, Stephen, 2006. *Keepers of the Flame: Understanding Amnesty International.* Cornell University Press.

Iopkins, Elwood M., 2005. *Collaborative Philanthropies: What Groups of Foundations Can Do that Individual Funders Cannot.* Lexington Books, Boulder.

Keck, Margaret E. and Kathryn Sikkink, 1998. *Activists Beyond Borders: Advocacy Networks in International Politics.* Cornell University Press. Ithaca, NY.

Martens, Kerstin, 2005. *NGOs and the United Nations: Institutionalization, Professionalization, and Adaptation.* Palgrave-McMillan. New York.

McCloskey, J. Michael, 2005. *In the Thick of It: My Life in the Sierra Club.* Island Press. Washington.

McKinley, E.H. 1995. *Marching to Glory: The History of The Salvation Army in the United States, 1880-1992.* (Ch. 6) Williams B. Eerdmands Publishing Company. Cambridge and Grand Rapids.

Minnear, Larry and Weiss, Thomas, 1995. *Mercy Under Fire: War and the Global Humanitarian Community.* Westview. Boulder, CO.

Nagel, Stuart S Ed., 1994. *Eastern European Development and Public Policy.* St. Martin's Press.

http://news.target.com/phoenix.zhtml?c=196187&p=irol-newsarticle&ID=932586, Accessed June 2007.

"NGOs in Consultative Status with ECOSOC" Department of Economic and Social Affairs. http://ww.un.org/esa/coordination/ngo/about.html, Accessed June 2005.

Oliner, Samuel P. 2003. *Do Unto Others: Extraordinary Acts of Ordinary People.* Westview Press.

Pease, Kelly-Kate S., 2000. *International Organizations: Perspectives on Governance in the Twenty-First Century*. Prentice Hall. New Jersey.

Raven, Peter H., 1990. "AIBS News: The Politics of Preserving Biodiversity." *Bioscience* 40, No. 10. November, 771.

Richmond, Oliver P. Ed., 2005. And Henry F. Carey. *Subcontracting Peace: The Challenges of NGO Peacebuilding*. Ashgate.

Rodrigues, Maria Guadalupe Moog, 2004. *Global Environmentalism and Local Politics: Transnational Advocacy Networks in Brazil, Ecuador and India*. State University of New York Press.

Swarts, Frederick A, 2003. "NGOs and Environmental Conservation." From Hamad, Tajeldin, et al. *Culture of Responsibility and the Role of NGOs*. Continuum International Publishing Group.

Ticknet, Joel, Carolyn Rafensperger, and Nancy Myers, "The Precautionary Principle in Action: A Handbook First Edition." Science and Environmental Health Network. Accessed May 2003 from http://www,biotech-info.net/precautionary.html.

Willets, Peter, Ed., 1996. *The Conscience of the World: The Influence of Non-Governmental Organizations in the UN System*. Hurst. London.

200 NGOs in China: A Special Report from the China Development Brief. January, 2005.

Living More Efficiently

1. http://www.data360.org/dsg.aspx?Data_Set_Group_ID=757 (accessed May 28, 2016)
2. Rodgers, Heather, 2005. *The Hidden Life of Garbage*, The New Press.
3. Aumaitre,A.L and J.G. Boyazoglu, 2010, "A note on livestock production and consumption in Europe." European Association for Animal Production, Via Nomentana 134, Rome 00162 Italy
4. Wikipedia.org, accessed July 2010

5. Shah, A. 2010. "Beef," March 21, Accessed June 2010 from http://www.globalissues.org/article/240/beef
6.http://www.worldwatch.org/files/pdf/Livestock%20and%20Climate%20Change pdf (accessed Dec. 23, 2012).
7. Shah, A. 2010.
8.http://www.thirdworldtraveler.com/Global_Secrets_Lies/Myth_FoodScarcity.ht ml, Accessed June 2010.
9. Gabler R., Petersen J., and Trapasso L. 2007. *Essentials of Physical Geography*, 8th Ed. Thomson Brooks/Cole. Belmont, California.
10. Kim, et al (2015) "Eating the Drought," Los Angeles Times, May 28.
11. Kim, et al (2015)
12. Pan A, Sun Q, Bernstein AM; et al. Red meat consumption and risk of type 2 diabetes: 3 cohorts of US adults and an updated meta-analysis. *Am J Clin Nutr.* 2011;94(4):1088- 1096.
13. Micha R, Wallace SK, Mozaffarian D. Red and processed meat consumption and risk of incident coronary heart disease, stroke, and diabetes mellitus: a systematic review and meta-analysis. *Circulation.* 2010;121(21):2271-2283.
14. Zheng W, Lee SA. Well-done meat intake, heterocyclic amine exposure, and cancer risk. *Nutr Cancer.* 2009;61(4):437-446.
15. Fraser GE. Associations between diet and cancer, ischemic heart disease, and all-cause mortality in non-Hispanic white California Seventh-day Adventists. *Am J Clin Nutr.* 1999;70(3)(suppl):532S-538S.
16. Sinha R, Cross AJ, Graubard BI, Leitzmann MF, Schatzkin A. Meat intake and mortality: a prospective study of over half a million people. *Arch Intern Med.* 2009;169(6):562-571.
17. Freston, K. 2012. "A Vegan Diet (Hugely) Helpful Against Cancer" Huffington Post, Dec. 9. http://www.huffingtonpost.com/kathy-freston/vegan-diet cancer_b_2250052.html?utm_hp_ref=fb&src=sp&comm_ref=false (accessed Dec.23, 2012).
18. Huffington Post. http://www.huffingtonpost.com/2012/01/06/ornish-diet-heart health-us-news_n_1188205.html (accessed Dec. 23, 2012).
19. Vandana Shiva, 2000, *Stolen Harvest*, South End Press, pp. 70-71.
20. http://www.bread.org/hunger/global/, Accessed on July 2010.
21. Hellmich, N., 2010, "U.S. obesity rate leveling off, at about one-third of adults." *USA Today* 1/13/2010. Accessed in June 2010 from: http://www.usatoday.com/news/health/weightloss/2010-01-13-obesity-rates_N.htm
22. McCandless, D. "Information is beautiful," *Above Magazine: for the Earth.* Spring 2010, UK.
23. Federal Trade Commission statistics, Accessed in July 2010 from http://www.ftc.gov/opa/2003/06/2001cigrpt.shtm

24. McGovern, G. 2001. "The Real Cost of Hunger," Accessed June 2010 from http://www.thefreelibrary.com/The+real+cost+of+hunger-a086062268

25. http://www.thirdworldtraveler.com/Global_Secrets_Lies/Myth_FoodScarcity.html, Accessed June 2010.

26. http://www.thirdworldtraveler.com/Global_Secrets_Lies/Myth_FoodScarcity.html, Accessed June 2010.

27. McGovern, G., 2001 "The Real Cost of Hunger,"

28. http://www.data360.org/dsg.aspx?Data_Set_Group_Id=757 (accessed May 28, 2016).

29. Schwartz, G. 1998 "Las Vegas, Baby: escaping reality and glimpsing the future in America's most infamous city." MS thesis, University of Wisconsin, Madison, Geography Dept.

30. http://www.water-ed.org/watersources/community.asp?rid=8&cid=524, Accessed May 2010.

31. http://ca.water.usgs.gov/groundwater/gwatlas/valley/landsub.html, Accessed June 2010

32. http://ca.water.usgs.gov/groundwater/gwatlas/valley/landsub.html, Accessed June 2010

33. http://www.globalchange.umich.edu/globalchange2/current/lectures/freshwater supply/freshwater.html, Accessed June 2010.

34. http://www.aph.gov.au/library/pubs/rn/2006-07/07rn12.pdf, accessed July 2010.

35. Taken from documentary film "Who Killed the Electric Car?" 2006.

36. "Who Killed the Electric Car?" 2006.

37. Costanza, B., 2001 "GM sues California's smog board." CBSmarketwatch.com, 24 Feb. Accessed June 2010.

38. 1997 U. S. tax code (section 179), http://www.hybridcenter.org/hybrid-vs-hummer.html, Accessed July 2010.

39. Energy Policy Act of 1992 (PL 103-486), http://www.hybridcenter.org/hybrid-vs-hummer.html, Accessed July 2010.

40. Curlee, T. Randal. Schexnayder, Vogt, Wolfe, Kelsay, and Feldman, 1994. *Waste to Energy in the United States: A social and economic assessment.* Quorum Books: 2.

41. Sayers, Dorothy L., 1942. "Why Work?"

42. http://www.tufts.edu/tuftsrecycles/USstates.htm, Accessed October, 2008.

43. http://hopebuilding.pbworks.com/Biogas-plants-in-Rwandan-prisons-treat-sewage,-generate- biogas-and-crop-fertilizer,-and-save-trees, Accessed July 2010.

44. http://www.calrecycle.ca.gov/LGCentral/Library/innovations/ recoverypark/CaseStudies1.htm, Accessed July 2010.

45. California IWMB. "Taking Packaging for Granted: Can you afford to? 2007": 2.

Other Sources:

Biocycle Magazine Annual Survey, 2004.

California Integrated Waste Management Board. "Feasibility Study on the Expanded Use of Agricultural and Forest Waste in Commercial Product. January 1999."

California Integrated Waste Management Board. "Last Chance Mercantile: A model for local government recycling and waste reduction. 2002": 1.

California Integrated Waste Management Board "Organics Options: opportunities for local government reuse, recycling, and composting. 2002": 1.

Dickerson, M., 2010. "Tokyo's goal: Be the greenest." *Los Angeles Times*, April 23.

Key T.J., Fraser G.E., Thorogood M.; et al. Mortality in vegetarians and nonvegetarians: detailed findings from a collaborative analysis of 5 prospective studies. *Am J Clin Nutr.* 1999;70(3)(suppl):516S-524S.

Kreith, Frank, Ed., 1994. *Handbook of Solid Waste Management.* McGraaw-Hill.

Ornish, Dean. Holy Cow! What's Good For You Is Good For Our Planet: comment on "Red Meat consumption and Mortality." *Arch Intern Med.* Published online March 12, 2012. doi:10.1001/archinternmed.2012.17 U.S. EPA, 1989. "The Solid Waste Dilemma: An Agenda for Action." Office of Solid Waste and Emergency Response. EPA/530-SW-89-019, February.

Yen, T.F. Ed., 1974. *Recycling and Disposal of Solid Wastes: Industrial, agricultural, domestic.* Ann Arbor Science Publishers.

The Gift of Tragedy

1. Quotation by Osama Bin Laden. "Verbatim," *Time* Magazine, February 8, 2010, pg. 15.

2. http://pages.prodigy.net/unohu/brainwaves.htm#Alpha, accessed September 14, 2010.

Practical Suggestions for Taking Action

1. Fishman, C, 2006, "How Many Light Bulbs Does it Take to Change the World? One, and You're Looking at It." Fast Company Magazine, September 1, 2010. Viewed on Sept 29, 2010 at www.fastcompany.com/magazine/108/open_lightbulbs.html

23360971R00131

Made in the USA
San Bernardino, CA
24 January 2019